LEGAL LONDON

A PICTORIAL HISTORY

Extract from John Rocque's map of the Cities of London and Westminster, 1746, showing London Bridge and parts of the City of London and Southwark

This map also includes many of the places or sites featured in this book. Poultry (the location of one of the City Compters) runs east from Cheapside, upon which is the church of St Mary le Bow. One can see London Bridge, the gateway to Southwark. The Marshalsea and the King's Bench Prison are marked, on the east side of 'The Borough'. The map also includes Clink Street, the site of the Clink Prison, near the south bank of the Thames, west of the bridge.

LEGAL LONDON

A PICTORIAL HISTORY

MARK HERBER

PHILLIMORE

1999

Published by
PHILLIMORE & CO. LTD.
Shopwyke Manor Barn, Chichester, West Sussex

ISBN 1 86077 111 4

Printed and bound in Great Britain by
BIDDLES LTD.
Guildford, Surrey

CONTENTS

LIST OF ILLUSTRATIONS

Endpapers: Extract from John Rocque's map of the cities of London and Westminster, 1746, showing the Inns of Court, Holborn, Fleet Street and the Strand.
Frontispiece: Extract from John Rocque's map of the cities of London and Westminster, 1746, showing London Bridge and parts of the City of London and Southwark.

FOREWORD

by Lord Woolf, Master of the Rolls

Both the law and London have been changing with increasing rapidity. Lawyers are constantly moving to ever larger offices. The barristers are flowing out of Inns into the surrounding area. Chambers are getting larger and larger. The courts are expanding as well. Old courts are being replaced by new. New courts are being added to existing courts. The procedures within the courts are changing equally rapidly. We are embarking on the age of information technology. The concept of a paperless court no longer seems fanciful.

In the midst of all this change, it is very easy to forget our historical roots and the charm of old legal London. This book is a wonderful amalgam of the nostalgic records of a bygone period and an insight into the contemporary legal scene. Browsing through the attractive illustrations brings alive memories of some historic buildings which are alas no more and others which are still flourishing today. It is a great pleasure to be guided through its pages and for legal London to come alive thanks to the elegance of the descriptions.

I am sure *Legal London* will give great pleasure to many. Mr. Herber is to be congratulated on a significant achievement.

ACKNOWLEDGEMENTS

I must first thank Jeremy Smith of Guildhall Library for his very valuable assistance in locating particular illustrations that were vital for the completeness of this book and for his help in arranging the reproduction of sections of the map by John Rocque. Mr. Roy Heywood of Wildy & Sons also assisted me in locating some of the prints that are reproduced here. Mr. R. Aspinall, Librarian of the Museum of Docklands, located the photograph at illustration 61. Mr. Keith Harrison was kind to supply me with the postcards of the interior of Newgate Gaol. Eva Yocum of the Museum of London was also very helpful in my search for important illustrations.

I have had the benefit of two splendid encyclopaedias of London, noted in the bibliography: one by William Kent and the other by Ben Weinreb and Christopher Hibbert. These works should be on the bookshelves of anyone interested in London history. Some of the illustrations in this work are reproduced from *Old and New London* and *Wonderful London*, also noted in the bibliography.

I would also like to express my gratitude to Lord Woolf, Master of the Rolls, for kindly agreeing to write the foreword. I would also thank the following for their permission to reproduce certain of the illustrations in this book:

Illustrations 22, 48, 52-54, 59, 65, 127, 180, 182, 183, 199, 200, 204-8, 213, 214, 218 and 229 and the maps appearing as the endpapers and the frontispiece: Guildhall Library, Corporation of London; illustrations 34, 46, 202, 210, 212, 222, 223 and 225: Museum of London; illustration 61: Museum of London, PLA Collection; illustration 47: Mirror Syndication International; illustration 57: The Hulton Getty Picture Collection; illustrations 141 and 142: El Vino Company Ltd.; illustration 144: The Treasurer and Masters of the Bench of Lincoln's Inn (photograph, Courtauld Institute of Art); illustrations 169-71: the partners of Allen & Overy.

INTRODUCTION

1999 is an important year for many reasons. It is not only the last year of the century, but of the millennium. This year has seen the sad passing of Lord Denning, aged 100, probably the best known lawyer of this century. 1999 can therefore be seen as the end of an era. However, it can also be seen as the dawn of a new era. Changes within the legal profession are occurring much more rapidly than before; solicitors have been gaining rights of audience in the higher courts, lawyers now have computers on their desks, mobile phones in their hands and a legal library on a few CD-ROMs. Proceedings can be issued from a court by use of the fax machine. Judges or Masters can conduct hearings by telephone or video-conferencing with the parties' solicitors. 1999 has also seen the most substantial changes in the procedural rules for civil litigation since the 19th century.

So this is also a good time to look back. London was the birthplace of the Common Law, which has flourished and spread to so many other countries around the world. It remains the most important centre of the Common Law countries, and so it deserves a tribute to its place in legal history.

I have generally limited this pictorial history to the period prior to 1939 yet, even so, there remain so many aspects to Legal London that it has proved impossible to include all I wished into one book. Buildings, institutions, people and ephemera; civil and criminal law; secular and ecclesiastical institutions; Judges and the judged; the Temple and the prisons – there is so much to cover that many aspects of Legal London have had to be omitted.

London's importance to the law arose principally from the location there, from Norman times, of the principal law-making institutions for England; the King's Council, the Houses of Parliament and the Royal Courts (first at Westminster, then on the Strand). This resulted in many lawyers living in London, or lodging in London during the law terms. It also resulted in the great institutions of the English legal profession developing in London; the Inns of Court and the Inns of Chancery. This process continued into the 19th and 20th centuries. The Law Society was founded in London and most of the large, international, firms of solicitors that have developed this century, are based in London.

This book is not limited to national legal institutions, but also covers London's own institutions; in the City of London, the City of Westminster, and in those areas now within Greater London, such as Southwark (originally in Surrey) and Clerkenwell (originally in Middlesex). The charter of Henry I to the City of London granted the City the right to elect its own justices. This is the foundation of the City's privilege of holding trials of Crown pleas in the chief court of criminal justice in England – now the Central Criminal Court in Old Bailey. In addition, there are courts that are specifically for London; the courts at Guildhall and the Lord Mayor's Court at Mansion House.

There have been many prisons within London and I have included illustrations of most of them. There are also sections devoted to the police and to the lawyers who undertook the application and administration of the law in London. I should, however, include here an explanation of the terms used to describe members of the legal profession over the centuries. The profession today consists principally of solicitors, barristers and the judges. A solicitor is a general practitioner of the law and an officer of the court who is instructed by members of the public to act, generally for a fee, in their legal business. A barrister acts as an advocate in the higher law courts (although solicitors have also recently obtained the right to be appointed as advocates in these courts). A judge is an officer of the Crown who is appointed to hear and decide cases in the law courts. Judges are appointed principally from the ranks of barristers, although an increasing number of solicitors are also elevated to the judiciary.

How did these distinctions arise? In Norman times, a dispute before a court required the personal attendance of the parties. By the early 13th century, it became possible for a litigant to appoint a legal representative, or agent, in a court and this right was gradually extended to all types of court action. This agent was known as an attorney. As the law developed, so it became important that an attorney had technical knowledge as to the law and the increasingly complicated procedural aspects of a court case. The clerks of some of the courts commonly acted as attorneys for litigants, but other men worked in or near the courts, gaining expertise in law and procedure, and offering to act as attorneys to those who would pay them to do so. A litigant might also require someone with particular eloquence and knowledge to speak on his behalf at court – a professional pleader or advocate. Men offering such a service also appeared in the 13th century. The Statute of Westminster of 1275 recognised that men were providing legal services for fees and that they should be subject to some control by the courts. The practice of attorneys and pleaders being appointed, or admitted to act, in each of the Royal Courts developed over the next century. The City of London already had its own system of courts and provision was made in 1290 for attorneys to be admitted each year, to act in particular courts, by the Lord Mayor.

At this time, the legal profession had not yet divided into two distinct branches. An attorney might plead a case in court and a pleader might consult directly with a client. Lawyers were also organising themselves into societies in London, within easy reach of the Royal Courts. Their motives were social and professional – lodging, dining, discipline and training. These societies developed into the Inns of Court and Inns of Chancery, and membership was not limited to pleaders, but extended to attorneys and court officials and clerks. However, the distinctions between attorneys and pleaders increased. As legal proceedings became more complex, the art of pleading required more special training and experience. The pleaders therefore left the mechanical work of a court action to attorneys. In the 14th and 15th centuries, the Inns of Court acquired the exclusive privilege of granting men the right to plead in the Royal Courts, by calling men to the Bar (and the term Barrister thus arose around 1530). In the 15th century, further steps were also taken to ensure that only suitable men, as regards character and legal knowledge, acted as attorneys. The procedures for each court to appoint attorneys were tightened up and provision was made for attorneys to be examined by the court and to swear to serve faithfully in their office. The role of the solicitor should also be mentioned here. A solicitor was someone who would solicit, urge or agitate. The attorneys employed such men to carry out business on their behalf; particularly in the court offices.

The 15th and 16th centuries saw the rise of the Courts of Equity, the most famous being the Court of Chancery, which were intended to remedy the defects and technicalities of actions in the courts of Common Law. New prerogative courts also appeared; the best known being the Court of Star Chamber. At first, only the court clerks were permitted to act as attorneys in these courts (in Chancery, there were the Six Clerks). However, there was too much business for them to handle and the problem was not solved by the appointment of up to ten under-clerks for each of the Six Clerks. Litigants needed expert help to ensure that their cases were progressed and these men were called common solicitors – that is men who would solicit, urge or agitate, but on behalf of anyone who would pay their fees, rather than on behalf of one attorney. The solicitors were not officers of the court. They were not 'admitted' to a court and were subject to little regulation. An act of 1605 simply required that they be of sufficient and honest disposition. Any man could act as a common solicitor and the reputation of this group was very poor. However, their work was important and by the 17th century, the common solicitors were undertaking, in the Court of Chancery, very similar work to that of the attorneys in the courts of Common Law.

The distinctions between pleaders and attorneys (or solicitors) deepened. Orders excluding attorneys and solicitors from their membership were made by Middle Temple in 1555, Lincoln's Inn in 1556 and the Inner Temple in 1557 (and this would exclude them from being called to plead before the Royal Courts). The judges controlled the admission of attorneys at the courts and, concerned to ensure they were trained and subject to the supervision of their peers, pressed that attorneys should remain as members of either Inns of Court or the Inns of Chancery. In practice, many members of the Inns did continue to work as attorneys. The policy of exclusion therefore only became truly effective in the 18th century after the Inns of Court had repeated the exclusion orders and also hindered attorneys using their membership of an Inn to train as barristers. The Inns required that there be a gap between a man ceasing to act as an attorney and being called to the Bar through one of the Inns. This required a cessation of income for any attorney wishing to transfer to the Bar. In contrast, the distinctions between the Common Law attorneys and the solicitors of Equity were being eroded. Many men acted as both attorneys and solicitors and an act of 1729 set out the same regulations for admission for either group, and confirmed that an attorney might be admitted as a solicitor in Chancery. In 1749, solicitors became automatically entitled to become attorneys. The distinction between attorneys and solicitors was now purely formal and that came to an end in 1875, with the fusion of Equity and Common Law.

There is much more that could be said about the history of the legal profession. The developments of the last few years are of particular interest. The split between the branches of the profession is gradually becoming eroded. However, there are many detailed works on these matters, some noted in the bibliography. It is time for us to turn back to the 11th century.

1 THE TOWER OF LONDON:
FORTRESS, PRISON AND PLACE OF EXECUTION

The Tower of London is London's most famous fortification. The keep was commenced by William I and completed in about 1097. It became known as the White Tower in the 13th century, when its walls were whitewashed. The Tower of London extends to 13 acres and has been used as a prison (particularly for political or religious prisoners), a court and a place of execution. However, the Tower has also housed the Crown Jewels, the Crown's armoury, State records, the Mint, as well as a reliable garrison and a menagerie. Cells were built in the original keep and the first recorded prisoner was Ranulf Flambard, bishop of Durham, in 1101. A separate gaol was built by Henry II. John Baliol, King of the Scots, was a prisoner here in 1296. About 600 Jews were imprisoned in the Tower in 1278, on false charges of clipping coins. Some were executed and many others died in the dungeons (the Jewish population was expelled from England in 1290). Henry VI was imprisoned in the Tower in 1464 and murdered there in 1471. The Duke of Clarence was imprisoned in the Tower in 1478 for plotting against his brother Edward IV and died, possibly in a 'butt of Malmsey'. Edward V and Richard, Duke of York, the sons of Edward IV, were held in the Tower from 1483 and then disappeared (probably murdered) between that year and 1485. Controversy still rages as to whether the culprit was Richard III, the Duke of Buckingham or Henry VII (my vote is for Buckingham). Sir Thomas More was held in the Bell Tower before his execution in 1534/5. Philip Howard, son of the Duke of Norfolk, died in the Tower in 1595, having been a prisoner for 10 years. Sir Walter Raleigh spent most of his 13 years' imprisonment in the Tower. Lord Grey died in the Tower after 11 years' imprisonment, for his part in a plot to place Arabella Stuart on the throne. Archbishop Laud was imprisoned in the Tower in 1641 and executed there in 1645. The Duke of Monmouth was held in the Tower in 1685, before his execution on Tower Hill. The notorious Judge Jeffreys was imprisoned in the Tower in 1688 and died there in 1689. Thomas Hardy was imprisoned for four months in 1794. William Joyce ('Lord Haw-Haw') was imprisoned in the Tower as recently as 1945, awaiting execution for treason. Torture was a popular pastime in the Tower (Guy Fawkes was racked before signing his confession). The Tower was sometimes used for sittings of courts. Itinerant Justices sat at the Tower for the Eyre (the predecessor of Assize Courts) of London in 1244 and 1276. The Justices dealt with the cases of any prisoners, received reports of any wrongdoing in the area and coroner's reports on any recent sudden deaths.

1

The Tower of London
This photograph shows the White Tower at the centre, high above the other buildings within the walls.

2

Traitors' Gate at the Tower of London
Traitors' Gate was the entrance to the Tower from the River Thames, and the convenient entrance for

The Tower of London. Traitors' Gate.

3

The place of execution on Tower Green
This view shows the site of the scaffold, surrounded by a railing, with the Chapel of St Peter ad Vincula in the background. Queen Anne Boleyn was beheaded here, or nearby, in 1536. Margaret, Countess of Salisbury, the last of the Plantagenets, was executed in 1541. She was 71 years old and it is said that she refused to lay her head on the block but was pursued around the block by the executioner until he hacked her to death with his axe. Queen Catherine Howard was beheaded in 1542, Lady Jane Grey in 1554 and Robert Devereux, Earl of Essex in 1601. Executions were carried out in other places in, or near, the Tower. Richard III was said to have had Lord Hastings beheaded on a log close to the White Tower. Tower Hill was a little to the north west of the Tower. Simon Sudbury, the Archbishop of Canterbury, was captured by Wat Tyler's rebels in 1381 and executed there. Others who were beheaded on Tower Hill include Edward, Duke of Buckingham in 1521, Sir Thomas More in 1535, Thomas Cromwell in 1540, the Duke of Northumberland in 1553, Thomas Wentworth, Earl of Strafford in 1641, the Duke of Monmouth in 1685 and Lord Lovat (aged 80) in 1747. He was not the last person to be executed at Tower Hill (three of the Gordon rioters were hanged there in 1780), but he was the last to be beheaded there. In fact, he was the last man to be executed by beheading in England.

those prisoners arriving by water from their trials in the courts at Westminster. Many famous people passed through, rarely to return to freedom. They included Anne Boleyn, the second wife of Henry VIII, who was accused of adultery and imprisoned in the Tower in 1536. Other arrivals included Sir Thomas More in 1534, Thomas Cromwell in 1540, Queen Catherine Howard in 1542 and Lady Jane Grey in 1554. Princess Elizabeth passed through the gates in 1554, suspected of complicity in plots against her half-sister Mary, but she was subsequently released. Traitors' Gate was removed from the Tower in Victorian times and purchased by Phineas Barnum, an American showman.

4

Execution block and axe at the Tower of London
The axe is said to have been at the Tower since 1687.

II THE MOTHER OF PARLIAMENTS

For centuries, supreme legislative and judicial power lay at Westminster. The Crown, the House of Lords and the House of Commons produced legislation for the lawyers to apply, dissect and argue over. The Judicial Committee of the House of Lords, consisting of the Lord Chancellor and the Lords of Appeal in Ordinary, remains the final appeal court of the United Kingdom, and sits in rooms in Westminster. The Judicial Committee of the Privy Council also sat at Westminster (but now at 1 Downing Street) as a final court of appeal for some Commonwealth countries and the ecclesiastical courts. Trials of certain matters (for example, peerage claims) also took place in the Houses of Lords and Commons. The courts that sat in Westminster Hall are considered in the following section.

5
The Houses of Parliament from the south bank of the Thames
Much of the Palace of Westminster was destroyed by fire in 1834. This postcard shows the new Palace in the early years of the 20th century.

THE HOUSES OF PARLIAMENT, LONDON.

6
The chamber of the House of Lords
The House of Lords originally met in the White Chamber in the Palace of Westminster and then in the White Hall. This was too small and so the Lords moved to another hall that had previously been used by the Court of Requests. This hall was destroyed in the fire of 1834. New Houses of Parliament were built; the chamber of the House of Lords opening in 1847. This postcard of the chamber is from about 1930.

7
The chamber of the House of Commons
In the 16th century, the royal chapel of St Stephen at Westminster became the meeting place of the House of Commons. It was destroyed in the fire of 1834 and a new chamber for the Commons opened in 1851. The chamber was completely destroyed during the Blitz, on the night of 10-11 May 1941, but a new chamber was built. This postcard shows the pre-1941 chamber.

III THE ROYAL COURTS AT WESTMINSTER AND ON THE STRAND

The Palace of Westminster was the principal royal residence in London from the reign of Edward the Confessor until the reign of Henry VII. Westminster Hall, or the 'New Palace', was built in about 1097 by William Rufus and splendidly rebuilt by Richard II. It is the only surviving part of the original Palace. The Hall was used for banquets and, from the 13th century, it also housed the Royal Courts. William Wallace was tried here in 1305. Other famous trials include that of Sir Thomas More in 1535, Guy Fawkes and his confederates in 1606, Charles I in 1648 and Warren Hastings (whose trial lasted seven years) from 1788 to 1795.

The Supreme Court of Judicature now consists of the Court of Appeal (Civil and Criminal Divisions), the High Court of Justice (principally for civil cases) and the Crown Court (for criminal cases). Less important cases are heard in the separate County Courts (for civil actions) or Magistrates Courts (criminal cases). The High Court of Justice has three divisions – Queen's Bench, Chancery and Family. Judges of the Queen's Bench also conduct the most important criminal trials in the Crown Court.

The lineage of the Supreme Court should be described. The King's Council ('Curia Regis') met in Westminster Hall from Norman times. From the 12th century, various courts developed from the Council to deal with petitions and other judicial business that arose. The Court of King's Bench originally dealt with cases affecting either the monarch in person or the King's Peace. This jurisdiction gradually extended to cover most civil (and some criminal) matters. This court is the predecessor of the Queen's Bench Division of the High Court. The Court of Common Pleas evolved from the Council in the late 12th century. It dealt with the usual or 'common' suits that arose between the King's subjects, such as debts or disputes over land. It became the Common Pleas Division of the High Court in 1875 and was merged into the Queen's Bench Division in 1880. The King's Exchequer supervised the collection of tax and it developed its own court, the Court of Exchequer, that originally dealt with disputes over Crown revenues. It gradually extended its jurisdiction to disputes between individuals on many subjects. It became the Exchequer Division of the High Court in 1875 and was merged into the Queen's Bench and Chancery Divisions in 1880. Application of the Common Law to a dispute often led to an unfair result. The Common Law would not generally enforce trusts or grant an injunction and so aggrieved subjects might petition the King for justice to be done. Further courts developed to deal with these petitions. The most important was the Lord Chancellor's own court, the Court of Chancery, that was intended to apply rules of justice, or 'equity', to overcome the injustices of the Common Law. The Court of Chancery became the Chancery Division of the High Court in 1875.

There were other Royal Courts, some of which should be briefly mentioned. A Court of Requests, intended for poor litigants, sat from about 1493 to 1642. The Court of Wards and Liveries was established by Henry VIII to look after the estates of the Crown's tenants-in-chief who died leaving children who became royal wards until reaching maturity. The Court of Star Chamber also developed out of the King's Council in the reign of Henry VII to deal with matters requiring the King's intervention. By the late 16th century, it dealt almost exclusively with criminal cases. The court was abolished in 1641. The High Court of Admiralty was established in the 14th century to deal with maritime disputes. In 1875, it became part of the Probate, Divorce and Admiralty Division of the High Court (then later part of the Queen's Bench Division). The proving of wills, or grant of administrations over the

estates of the deceased ('Probate') and most aspects of marriage, separation (and sex) were originally matters for the church courts. However, a secular Probate Court and a Court for Divorce and Matrimonial Causes were established in 1857 and became part of Probate, Divorce and Admiralty Division of the High Court in 1875. Both probate and matrimonial causes are now dealt with by the Family Division.

The Court of King's Bench and the Court of Chancery sat in Westminster Hall from the 13th to the 19th centuries and the Court of Common Pleas is recorded there from the 15th century. These courts originally all sat in the same hall, with only low wooden partitions between them. The Court of Exchequer also sat in Westminster Hall, but in a separate chamber. The Court of Requests sat nearby, in the White Hall. The Court of Common Pleas moved to a separate room in 1732 and proper courtrooms were constructed within the hall only in 1740.

8
Westminster Hall, *c.*1800
This drawing from *Old and New London*, based upon a print of 1808, shows the exterior of the Hall.

9
The interior of Westminster Hall
The Hall was 240 feet long, 67 feet wide and 92 feet high. This view shows the magnificent roof (which was restored shortly after WW1) that was added during the rebuilding of the hall by Richard II.

10

The first day of term in Westminster Hall

During term time, Westminster Hall was a busy, noisy place. There were judges, lawyers, clients and witnesses for a number of cases being heard at the same time. Members of the public had access to the hall and legal booksellers, haberdashers and other tradesmen also had stalls selling law books, maps, clothes and many other items. This drawing, from *Old and New London*, is based upon a print entitled 'The first day of term' published in 1739 (when only partitions separated the courts that were sitting in the hall). Throughout the hall, lawyers can be seen discussing matters with clients or witnesses. Two of them appear to have brought their dogs to court. The trade stalls are on the left.

11

The Star Chamber

When sitting in the Palace of Westminster, the King's Council often used a room that had a ceiling adorned by stars, and which became known as the Star Chamber. By the reign of Henry VII, the Council often sat in this room when considering the judicial business of the Council. These Council meetings developed into the Court of Star Chamber. The court dealt principally with seven matters; conspiracy, forgery, fraud, libel, maintenance, perjury and riot. It soon acquired a reputation for oppression; partly because a party before the court was not given any opportunity to cross-examine the witnesses brought against him. This infamous court was abolished in 1641 and the room was demolished in 1835. This drawing from *Old and New London* is based on a drawing of the room made just before its demolition.

12
The Law Courts at Westminster,
*c.*1880
Some of the Royal Courts moved out
of Westminster Hall (thus the Court
of Chancery began sitting in
Lincoln's Inn Hall during the
vacation) and new rooms to house
the courts were built in 1820. They
were designed by Sir John Soane and
built on the west side of Westminster
Hall (facing Parliament Square).
The Court of Exchequer moved out
of its rooms, near Whitehall, to these
new courts in 1820 and the Court of
King's Bench moved from
Westminster Hall to this building
soon afterwards. These courtrooms
survived the fire at Westminster in
1834 but were only used until 1882
(when the Royal Courts of Justice on
the Strand were opened) and
demolished in 1883. This view,
looking south towards Millbank,
shows the front of the building.

London,-the Law Courts

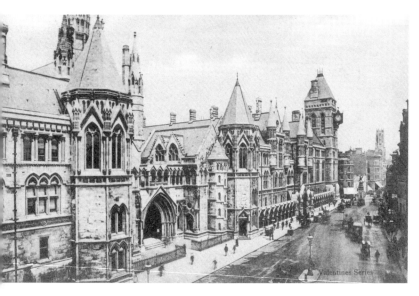

Valentines Series

Law Courts, Strand.
LONDON.

Four views of the Royal Courts of Justice on the Strand in the early 20th century

The seat of the Royal Courts of Justice is one of the most beautiful buildings in London. It was built between 1871 and 1882, to replace the courtrooms at Westminster, designed by G.E. Street and opened in 1882 by Queen Victoria. One problem during building was that Carey Street, which runs along the back of the courts, was 17 feet higher in level than the Strand. My favourite place, after the impressive main hall, is the 'Bear Garden', around which are the rooms of Masters and a Judge in Chambers. It is suggested that its name arose from the similarity of so many lawyers in such a small area to the bear-baiting that took place at Bear Gardens on Bankside and other places around London from the 13th century (until the 'sport' was banned in 1835). The building originally had 19 courts. Extensions have added another 16, together with further courtrooms for the Bankruptcy and Companies Courts. There are over 1,000 rooms and three miles of corridors. Although the courts here are predominantly for civil actions, there are cells in the basement for prisoners whose cases are being heard (for example by the Court of Appeal).

17

The statue of Gladstone on the Strand

William Ewart Gladstone (1809-98) is perhaps the best known of the 19th-century Prime Ministers, but he was also a member of Lincoln's Inn. Gladstone was first elected as a Conservative MP in 1832 and he entered Lincoln's Inn the following year. He served in Sir Robert Peel's governments and as Chancellor of the Exchequer in Lord Aberdeen's coalition government (1852-5) and in Lord Palmerston's government (1859-66). He became leader of the Liberal Party in 1867 and Prime Minister (1868-74, 1880-85, 1886 and 1892-94). This statue of Gladstone, in the robes of the Chancellor of the Exchequer, was unveiled at the west end of the Royal Courts of Justice in 1905. The statue stands on the same island as the church of St Clement Danes, looking towards Australia House on Aldwych.

Gladstone Statue in the Strand, London.

IV THE OTHER COURTS OF LONDON

There were many courts, or related buildings, in London, other than at Westminster. A selection of them is included here:

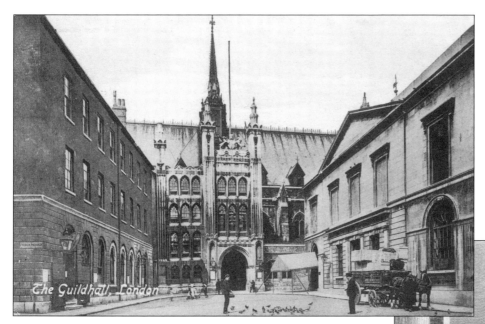

19 *(below)*
Guildhall, c.1828
This engraving was made from a drawing by Thomas Shepherd and published in 1828.

18 *(above)*
Guildhall in the City of London
Guildhall was the administrative centre of the City of London from the early 15th century. The Great Hall was built in about 1411, although there was a hall on the site from the 11th century. The Corporation of the City, consisting of the Lord Mayor, Sheriffs, Aldermen and Court of Common Council, have governed the Square Mile from here ever since. But the buildings also had a judicial function. The Guildhall was sometimes used for important London trials; such as the Earl of Surrey (in 1547) and Lady Jane Grey, her husband Lord Guildford Dudley and Archbishop Cranmer (1553/4). Dr. Lopez, a Spanish Jew and physician to Queen Elizabeth, was also tried here. He was accused of attempting to poison the Queen and hanged at Tyburn (1594). Henry Garnett was Superior of the Order of Jesuits in England. At his trial at Guildhall in 1606, he was accused of complicity in the Gunpowder plot and subsequently hanged. The City had a number of its own courts that sat here; the Court of Husting settled disputes between citizens and enrolled deeds or wills concerning transfers of property in the City. The court remains in existence, but rarely active. The Mayor's Court sat from the 13th century to deal with the overflow of business from the Husting Court. There were two Magistrates Courts for the City (one sitting at Guildhall and the other at Mansion House). Each Sheriff held a court at his Compter (a prison). These courts were transferred to Guildhall, united into the City of London Court in 1867, and amalgamated with the Mayor's Court in 1921. The Mayor's and City of London Court now acts as a County Court for the City. A Court of Requests was established in 1517, to deal with small debts. Its jurisdiction was transferred to the Sheriffs' Courts in 1847. There was also a Court of Orphans, which had custody of the orphans of freemen of the City and supervised the administration of their estates. The Great Hall was damaged in the Great Fire of London in 1666, but repaired. The front of Guildhall was reconstructed in 1789. Much was destroyed during WW2, but part of the Great Hall, in the centre of this picture, survives. The building on the left was the Justice Room, built in the 18th century, but demolished in 1972. Guildhall Library now stands on its site. This postcard dates from about 1913.

20 *(above)*

The Court of Requests of the City of London, Guildhall, *c.*1817
The Common Council of the City established its own Court of Requests in 1517. This engraving, published by Robert Wilkinson in 1817, shows the court sitting in the chapel of St Mary Magdalen at Guildhall. The chapel was built in the 14th century and used for worship by the Lord Mayor and officers of the Corporation. They attended St Lawrence Jewry from 1782 and the Guildhall Chapel was then converted to a courtroom. It was demolished in 1822.

21

Mansion House: the residence of the Lord Mayor of London
Lord Mayors originally used their own houses (or hired rooms) for their official duties. Mansion House was the first official home for the Lord Mayor, completed in 1752 to a design by George Dance the elder. It included a Justice Room, in which sat one of the Magistrates Courts for the City.

22

A hearing of a case by the Lord Mayor in the Justice Room at Mansion House
This engraving shows a hearing before the Lord Mayor and Alderman Farebrother, sitting as Magistrates of the City of London, in Mansion House in February 1844. This Magistrates Court dealt with offences committed in the City, south of a line drawn between Leadenhall Street and Holborn Viaduct. There were several cells below the court to hold prisoners awaiting the hearing of their case. Each ward of the City of London elects an alderman. Each alderman is a Justice of the Peace within his own ward or sits at the Magistrates Courts at Mansion House and Guildhall. On this occasion, William Barber, Joshua Fletcher, Georgina Dorey and Thomas Griffin were examined by the Lord Mayor and Alderman on charges of forging wills and obtaining fraudulent transfers of stock. The four were remanded in custody pending their trials in the next Sessions.

St Mary-le-Bow, Cheapside: the seat of the Court of Arches of the Archbishop of Canterbury

Archdeacons, bishops and archbishops each had their own courts and jurisdictions. The Archbishop of Canterbury's court was named the Prerogative Court of Canterbury. The Archbishop rarely presided over it himself but delegated this task to his officials. Appeals from church courts in the Province of Canterbury (about two thirds of England) were made to the Archbishop's Court of Arches. Further appeal could be made (after the break with Rome) to the Court of Delegates. These appeals are now made to the Judicial Committee of the Privy Council. The church of St Mary-le-Bow stands on the corner of Cheapside and Bow Lane. It was built in the 11th century and was originally known as St Mary of the Arches, because it was built on arches (still visible in the crypt). The Court of Arches often sat here (and took its name from the church arches) from the late 12th century until the destruction of the church in the Great Fire of 1666. The Court then moved to Doctor's Commons (see illustration 25). The church was rebuilt by Wren and the Court of Arches still occasionally sits in its ancient seat. This view is from about 1900. The beautiful tower survived the Blitz. Most of the church was destroyed, but has been restored.

Lambeth Palace: the London residence of the Archbishop of Canterbury

The enormous role of the church in the law in previous centuries is often forgotten. The ecclesiastical courts did not deal only with religious affairs, such as prosecutions of people ('recusants') for failure to attend church, or with discipline of the clergy. The church courts dealt with many other matters that only gradually passed to the secular courts. Actions for defamation in the 16th century were more likely to be heard by church courts than by the Royal Courts. Wills were proved in church courts until 1858. The head of the church, apart from the monarch, was the Archbishop of Canterbury, and this postcard of about 1930 shows Lambeth Palace, the Archbishop's London residence. The earliest parts date from the 13th century, but much was built in the 15th century. There were dungeons in the Palace and cells in the Gatehouse (built by Cardinal Morton, Archbishop of Canterbury and Lord Chancellor from 1486 to 1500). Sir Thomas More was examined at Lambeth Palace in 1534 by Thomas Cromwell and others of the King's Council, after he refused to sign the Oath of Supremacy. He was then sent to the Tower. The Palace was used as a prison during the Civil War and Commonwealth.

The Prerogative Court of Canterbury in Doctors' Commons
From medieval times, ecclesiastical and admiralty (maritime) court actions were determined by civil and canon law, rather than the Common Law of England. The lawyers in these courts were originally clerics. The men who worked as advocates were required to obtain doctorates in civil law (that is Roman Law) from Oxford or Cambridge Universities. The equivalent of attornies in the ecclesiastical courts were Proctors (some of whom had bachelor degrees in canon or civil law from Oxford or Cambridge). The College of Advocates and Doctors of Law, known as Doctors' Commons, was a society of judges and advocates who were Doctors of Law and practised in the courts. The Society was founded in the late 15th century. The lawyers originally worked from a house in Paternoster Row, but later practised from chambers in two quadrangles in a building (a college or common house) also known as 'Doctors' Commons' in Knightrider Street, between the Thames and St Paul's Cathedral. The Proctors (regulated by the Archbishop of Canterbury) were also located here. The courts in which the Advocates and Proctors worked were spread around London; the Court of Arches was at St Mary le Bow, other London ecclesiastical courts sat at St Paul's Cathedral and at Southwark. The Court of Admiralty also sat at Southwark. The Archbishop of Canterbury's Prerogative Court (PCC) was the senior ecclesiastical court in which wills were proved and administrations granted. The principal office of the PCC was in Ivy Lane and the court often sat in St Paul's Cathedral. After the Great Fire of London, a courtroom was provided at Doctors' Commons for hearings of the ecclesiastical and admiralty cases. Five courts sat in Doctors' Commons; (1) the Court of Arches, (2) the Prerogative Court, (3) the Court of Faculties and Dispensations, (4) the Consistory Court of the Bishop of London and (5) the High Court of Admiralty. Charles Dickens worked as a shorthand writer in the courts at Doctors' Commons.

In 1857, a new court for Divorce and Matrimonial Causes was established. The probate jurisdiction of the ecclesiastical courts ended in January 1858 and a new, secular, Court of Probate and its Principal Probate Registry commenced work. Barristers could appear in these courts and the Doctors had thus lost most of their exclusive areas of work within one year. They dissolved their society. Some joined the Inns of Court and became barristers. Most of the buildings of Doctors' Commons were demolished in 1867. This engraving, from a drawing by Thomas Shepherd, shows the front of the Prerogative Court's offices. A Registrar and clerks dealt with storing and recording the wills and administrations, and the court dealt with disputes that arose.

PREROGATIVE WILL OFFICE

26
The interior of the Prerogative Office in Doctors' Commons

27
Beating of the bounds of the parish of All Hallows, Barking-by-the-Tower; Ascension Day 1933
This custom was for the parish beadle and churchwardens to lead the priest and people of a parish around the boundaries of a parish to confirm them. It was also custom to bump charity school boys into walls at the boundary (or beat them with willow wands at places where no walls existed) to make them remember the boundaries.

28

Somerset House and St Mary-le-Strand

A palace was built 1547-50 on the north bank of the Thames for the Protector (Edward Seymour, the Duke of Somerset) during the reign of Edward VI. It was demolished in 1775. The original church of St Mary-le-Strand was demolished on the orders of the Protector in 1549, probably because it interfered with the view from his new palace. The new church of St Mary-le-Strand was not built until 1714-7 (and consecrated in 1724). The present

Somerset House, on the same site as the Protector's Palace, was built between 1776 and 1786 as Government offices, such as the Navy Pay Office and the Stamp Office, and it was also used by various learned societies, such as the Society of Antiquaries. This is an engraving of that building from a drawing by Thomas Shepherd. Somerset House became important to lawyers. Wills proved, and administrations granted, in the Principal Probate Registry of the secular courts since 1858 were held at Somerset House until early 1999

(together with copies of all wills and administrations from local probate registries in England and Wales). The Registrar General, responsible for the civil registration of births, marriages and deaths since 1837, also had offices and search rooms at Somerset House from 1837 until 1973. Somerset House was also important to many lawyers and their clients because of the Board of Inland Revenue's offices there.

29

A view of Somerset House from Embankment

30

The College of Arms, *c*.1830
An engraving of the College of
Arms, also known as the College of
Heralds, from a drawing by Thomas
Shepherd, published in 1830. The
Heralds were a part of the Royal
Household from the 13th century.
They were granted a charter of
incorporation by Richard III in 1484
and the College now consists of four
Kings of Arms (Garter, Clarenceux,
Norroy and Ulster), six Heralds
(Windsor, Chester, Lancaster, York,
Richmond and Somerset) and four
Pursuivants (Rouge Croix,
Bluemantle, Rouge Dragon and
Portcullis). They act, under the
authority of the Crown and the Earl
Marshal (the Duke of Norfolk), to
control the grant and use of coats of
arms in England, Wales, Northern
Ireland and the Commonwealth.
The Heralds moved to the present
site in 1555, when Queen Mary
granted to them Derby House, a
London home of the Earls of Derby.
It was destroyed in the Great Fire of
London and a new college was built
in 1672-8 fronting on Bennet's Hill.
In 1867-8, part of the College was
pulled down to make way for Queen
Victoria Street, which now runs past
the entrance to the College. The
building was restored in 1877.

31

**A session of the Earl Marshal's
Court, the Court of Chivalry**
This drawing from *Old and New
London* is based upon a picture by
Rowlandson, published in
Ackerman's *Microcosm of London*. It
featured what was, at that time, the
last sitting of the Heraldic Court in
1737. The court did not then sit for
many years, until December 1954,
when it heard the case of 'The Lord
Mayor, Aldermen and Citizens of the
City of Manchester v. The
Manchester Palace of Varieties
Limited'. This concerned the
unauthorised use by an
entertainment hall of the City's coat
of arms. The court may still convene
to hear disputes over the use of coats
of arms or other heraldic regalia.

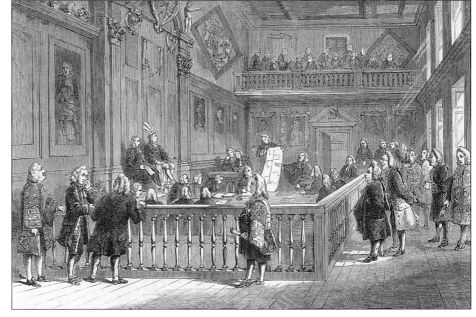

32
A case before the Court of Pie Powder of Bartholomew Fair
Bartholomew Fair was held every summer, for three days from the eve of St Bartholomew's Day (24 August) from about 1123 to 1855. It developed from the market (for livestock) held at Smithfield from the 11th century. Rahere (died 1143/4), the founder of St Bartholomew's Priory and church,

obtained Royal charters to establish the fair. It expanded, as years passed, to include all sorts of traders and amusements, such as wrestlers and fire-eaters. Bartholomew Fair, like many fairs, had its own court – a Court of Pie Powder. This was named from the French 'Pied-Poudres' (the 'dusty-footed' or 'travellers'). It had jurisdiction over commercial complaints or certain offences that arose out of the fair

(for example a theft, but only if the thief was captured within the bounds of the market). The Prior of St Bartholomew's originally presided over the court and a jury of traders would be empanelled. The court originally met within the Priory gates but later met at the *Hand and Shears Tavern* in Cloth Fair, behind St Bartholomew's. This engraving shows the tavern and the court in session.

33

The Sessions House in Old Bailey in 1750

Serious crimes in most of England were tried by itinerant justices at Assizes held in permanent or temporary courtrooms. The assize system did not apply to the City of London or Middlesex. Offenders were held in Newgate Gaol and there were eight annual sessions of the commissions of 'Oyer and Terminer' (to hear and determine) and of gaol delivery from Newgate. Until the 16th century, there was no specific courthouse for the trials, but the Sheriffs and Corporation of the City would hire rooms close to the prison. In 1539, the Court of Aldermen resolved to build a special courthouse in the Old Bailey for this purpose. The courts at this Sessions House then exercised criminal jurisdiction over London, Middlesex and parts of the adjoining counties. Both the Sessions House and Newgate Gaol were burnt down in the Great Fire. This drawing from *Old and New London* shows the Sessions House that was built after the fire (and used until 1774).

34

The Sessions House in Old Bailey in 1812

This engraving of 1812 shows the Sessions House built in 1774 on Old Bailey. Sweet-smelling herbs were strewn around the courts or carried in bouquets by judges to counter the unpleasant odours from Newgate Gaol next door. The sessions of 'Oyer and Terminer' and gaol delivery were abolished in 1834 and replaced by sittings of the Central Criminal Court, permanently located at the Sessions House (and later in the building known as the Central Criminal Court).

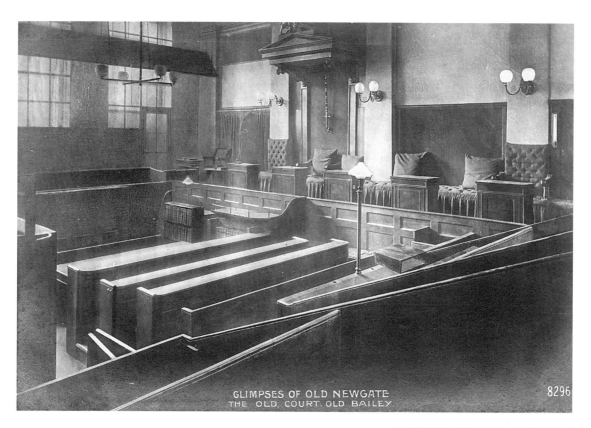

GLIMPSES OF OLD NEWGATE
THE OLD COURT, OLD BAILEY.

8296

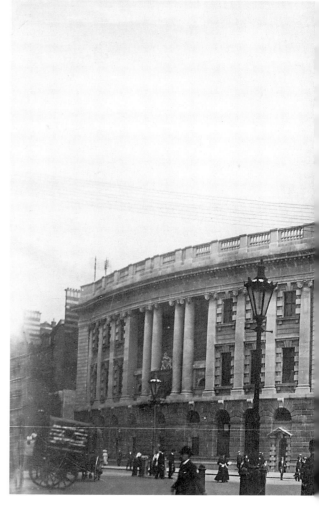

35 *(top)*

The interior of a court in the Sessions House in Old Bailey

This postcard shows the interior of the courtroom in the Sessions House in about 1896. In the centre is the Judge's canopy, with the Old Bailey sword hanging below it (a symbol of the authority of the Mayor). The box for the jurors is under the windows and faced by pews for the barristers. Part of the dock can be seen at the extreme left of the photograph. Oscar Wilde was tried in this building in 1895.

36 *(above)*

A trial at the Sessions House in Old Bailey

This engraving of about 1841, from a drawing by Thomas Shepherd, presents a slightly different angle from illustration 35; from behind the dock.

37 *(below)*
The Central Criminal Court, Old Bailey
Designed by Edward Mountford, the Central Criminal Court was opened in 1907 by Edward VII on the site of Newgate Gaol (demolished in 1902). This postcard shows the building soon after its completion, a view that is little changed today. On top of the dome is the figure of Justice with outstretched arms holding a sword and scales. The building contained four courtrooms, but now has 19. There are 70 cells for prisoners in custody. The building was damaged by bombs in 1940 and 1941 but restored. The resident judges are the Recorder and the Common Serjeant of London. Trials are also conducted by the Lord Chief Justice, High Court Judges and circuit judges. Famous trials here include that of Dr. Crippen and his mistress in 1910, William Joyce ('Lord Haw-Haw') in 1945, the Kray twins in 1969 and Peter Sutcliffe (the 'Yorkshire Ripper') in 1981.

The Central Criminal Courts, London.

38 *(above)*
The central hall of the Central Criminal Court

39
The interior of a courtroom at the Central Criminal Court
This is court number one; of similar appearance to the courtroom at the Sessions House (see illustration 35). The dock is on the right, masking most of the barristers' pews from view. The jury box is on the left, the table for solicitors in the centre and the judge's seat at centre rear.

40 *(left)*

Middlesex Guildhall, Westminster, c.1828

From 1689, and perhaps earlier, the Sessions for the City of Westminster were held in a building known as the City of Refuge (which attracted certain privileges of sanctuary until the Reformation). This building was demolished in 1775 and replaced in 1805 by the Guildhall of the City of Westminster, designed by Samuel Cockerell. The Guildhall is on the west side of (and faces) Parliament Square. This engraving of the building of 1805, from a drawing by Thomas Shepherd, was published in 1828. The Guildhall housed the Sessions for Westminster. It also housed the Royal Courts during repairs to Westminster Hall.

41 *(below left)*

Middlesex Guildhall, Westminster, c.1920

The Guildhall of 1805 was incorporated into a larger building in 1893 and rebuilt in 1913. This photograph shows the Guildhall after that rebuilding.

42

The Sessions House on Clerkenwell Green

This engraving of the Sessions House for Middlesex, from a drawing by Thomas Shepherd, was published in 1831. The Sessions House was built in 1779 to replace Hicks' Hall (demolished in 1777), a Sessions House built in about 1612 in St John Street by Sir Baptist Hicks, one of the Justices of the Peace for Middlesex. The Sessions of the Peace and Sessions of 'Oyer and Terminer' for Middlesex were then held at Clerkenwell Sessions House. It became notorious for the severe sentences imposed by the Judges and Magistrates who sat there. Additions were made to the building in 1860, 1876 and 1889. The Sessions removed to Newington Causeway, near the Elephant and Castle, in 1921 and the building is now the London Masonic Centre.

43
Bow Street Magistrates Court
Bow Street is the most famous of the
London Magistrates Courts. This
building, dating from 1881, has four
courts. The view in this postcard is
little changed today.

44
Marylebone Magistrates Court

45
**A hearing before the Court of
Chancery. The Lord Chancellor's
Court in the Old Hall of Lincoln's
Inn**
This is an engraving from a drawing
by Thomas Shepherd. The Court of
Chancery sat in Lincoln's Inn Old
Hall out of term time (the terms
then lasted only about 100 days in
total), from about 1734 until the
opening of the Royal Courts of
Justice in 1882. The Lord
Chancellor's Court (pictured here)
was joined in the hall in 1819 by the
Vice Chancellor's Court. A room for
a third court was built in 1841. The
Chancery Courts moved from
Lincoln's Inn to the Royal Courts of
Justice in the Strand in 1882.

V CRIME AND PUNISHMENT

Crime has always been a part of London life. The sparse records of medieval times contain many references to murders, fights, forgery and vagrancy. London was also the obvious centre for conspiracies, riots and revolts. Vagrants were attracted to London from throughout the kingdom by its wealth and relative anonymity. Southwark, with its brothels and bear-baiting pits, was notorious for crime and lawlessness. London had its thieves, robbers and gangs of criminals. In the 18th century, there were up to 6,000 shops selling cheap gin. Thousands of neglected children turned to crime to survive. Drunkenness, gambling and prostitution were rife. In the 19th century, it was estimated that London had 6,000 brothels and about 80,000 prostitutes. The criminal justice system was plagued by corruption – the rich or well connected might escape prosecution or punishment. The forces of law and order were inadequate to deal with day-to-day crime. A criminal might commit many crimes with little fear of detection, but if caught faced the prospect of a swift trial and violent punishment. There were many places of punishment or imprisonment in London. Only some can be shown here. Tower Hill and the Tower of London have already been noted. Other places of punishment included an open area by a fountain in Cheapside known as the Standard. Walter de Stapleton, Treasurer to Edward II, was beheaded there in 1326 and Jack Cade beheaded Lord Say there in 1450. A pillory (see illustration 52) was also placed there. Old London Bridge and its gatehouse (at the southern end of the bridge) were often adorned with heads (such as those of William Wallace, Jack Cade, Sir Thomas More, Thomas Cromwell and two alleged lovers of Queen Catherine Howard), dipped in tar to preserve them. The quarters of those executed might be displayed instead of their heads. A German visitor in 1592 noted about 30 heads rotting over the Gatehouse. New Palace Yard, on the north side of Westminster Hall, was also used for punishments. Perkin Warbeck was placed in the stocks there in 1498 and Titus Oates was pilloried in 1685. Executions also took place on Kennington Common (including many Scottish rebels in 1746). Pirates were hanged at Execution Dock, near Wapping New Stairs, as late as the 19th century.

46

A case being heard at Bow Street, c.1808
An aquatint by Pugin and Rowlandson, published in Ackerman's *Microcosm of London* in 1808. The original Magistrates Office at Bow Street was opened in 1739, by the first Bow Street magistrate, Sir Thomas de Veil, in his own house on the west side of Bow Street. The second Bow Street magistrate was Henry Fielding (barrister and the author of *Tom Jones*). His blind half-brother Sir John Fielding was also appointed in 1754. The inadequacy of the parish constables and watchmen caused Henry Fielding to establish a group of men as volunteer 'thief-takers', who received reward money for convictions they obtained. They became known as the 'Bow Street Runners'. They remained under the control of the Bow Street Magistrates after the establishment of the Metropolitan Police and were only disbanded in 1839, when the Magistrates Offices became Magistrates Courts and magistrates lost their responsibilities for police work. The courthouse of de Veil was replaced in 1881 by the present court (illustration 43) on the east side of Bow Street.

**47
Dr. Hawley Harvey Crippen and his mistress Ethel Le Neve in the dock at Bow Street in 1910**
Dr. Crippen is one of the most famous British murderers. Following the murder of Crippen's wife by poison (her body was found under the cellar of their house at 39 Hilldrop Crescent, Islington), Crippen and his mistress tried to escape to America on the SS *Montrose*. However, the liner's captain became suspicious of the couple (disguised as a father and son) and sent a 'radiogram' to alert Scotland Yard. The police took a faster vessel, overtook the *Montrose* and arrested them. Crippen was hanged in 1910 but Le Neve was found not guilty. This is a rare photograph of an accused in the dock. Photography in the courts was banned in 1925.

**48
Murder in Long Acre: the murder and dismemberment by Mary Aubrey of her husband in 1687**
No book on Legal London would be complete without a gruesome murder. This etching, published in 1798, shows Mary Aubrey, a midwife, murdering her husband in Long Acre, Westminster in 1687, by chopping off his head and limbs. She was hanged and then burned at Tyburn (as shown in the inset). Her son was acquitted.

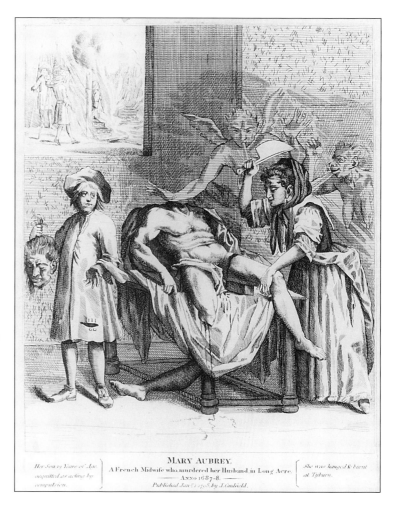

Her Son 12 Years of Age acquitted as acting by compulsion.

MARY AUBREY.
A French Midwife who murdered her Husband in Long Acre.
ANNO 1687-8.
Published Jan.º 1 1798 by J.Caulfield.

She was hanged & burnt at Tyburn.

49

Preparations for a burning at the place of execution in Smithfield
Smithfield was a grassy, open space outside the City walls with a celebrated horse and livestock market in the 12th century. Bartholomew Fair was also held there from the 12th century until 1855. The area was also used for sports, tournaments and, for over 400 years, public executions. Criminals were hanged until the 15th century, when the gallows at Tyburn became the preferred venue. However, many others continued to suffer at Smithfield by being boiled or burned alive. In 1530, John Roose, a cook, was boiled to death for having poisoned gruel made for the household of Bishop Fisher of Rochester – 17 people were poisoned and two died. In 1538, Prior John Forest was roasted alive, in a cage, for refusing to recognise Henry VIII as supreme head of the church. Under Queen Mary, at least 43 people (and perhaps as many as 200) were burned at Smithfield; seven in one day (27 June 1558). The first martyr was John Rogers, the vicar of St Sepulchre's Church (in 1554). In 1555, John Taylor, vicar of St Bride, Fleet Street was also burned. Under Edward VI, he had denied the ancient faith and declared that the sacrament was merely bread and wine. In Queen Mary's reign, he was committed to the Fleet Prison, then brought before a commission that sat in the Lady Chapel of St Mary Overies Church in Southwark. He was then confined in Bread Street Compter and in Newgate before he was burned in Smithfield on 30 May 1555. Burning at the stake continued for many years – the last time a woman was burned in England was in 1789 (outside Newgate Gaol) when Christian Murphy was burned (after hanging) for the offence of coining. This drawing is from *Old and New London*.

50
The grisly end for the Gunpowder Plot conspirators in 1605
In 1605, a Catholic named Guy Fawkes was found in a cellar of the Houses of Parliament at Westminster with gunpowder. He was tortured to reveal his fellow conspirators, including Robert Catesby, Thomas Winter, Robert Winter, Thomas Percy, Christopher Wright and John Wright. Catesby and Percy were killed by those arresting them. Fawkes and seven other conspirators were executed, five in St Paul's Churchyard and three at Westminster. This drawing, from *Old and New London* is based upon a print of 1795. The conspirators can be seen being dragged on hurdles through the streets to Old Palace Yard, to the south of Westminster Hall, then hanged, burned and disembowelled. Their heads were displayed on spikes. Sir Walter Raleigh was also executed in this yard in 1618.

51
The stocks and whipping post at St Leonard's, Shoreditch
It was common for people to be whipped or placed in the stocks, and so many parishes had their own stocks and whipping post. Statutes even prescribed whipping for unmarried mothers. The old stocks and whipping post of the parish of St Leonard's, Shoreditch were found among some lumber in the crypt of the church and placed in the churchyard under a canopy of thatch. The whipping post can be seen at the centre of the photograph, with manacles for the prisoner's hands.

52

**Daniel Defoe in the pillory at
Temple Bar**

From as early as the 13th century,
criminals might also be placed in the
pillory. The Statute of the Pillory of
1226 provided for it to be used for
perjurers, forgers and users of
deceitful weights and measures.
From the 17th century, it was also
used for those who libelled the
government or who published
without a licence. In 1783,
Christopher Atkinson M.P. was
placed in a pillory outside the Corn
Exchange in Mark Lane on
conviction for perjury (he was also
imprisoned for 12 months, expelled
from the House of Commons and
fined £2,000). Unpopular offenders
might be pelted by the crowds with
refuse or worse. Titus Oates was
convicted of perjury in 1685 (his

false evidence sent two innocent
men to the gallows) and sentenced
to be whipped and then placed in
the pillory outside Westminster Hall.
He was almost killed by the mob.
However, popular men were treated
very differently. This print shows
Daniel Defoe in a pillory (but
incorrectly near Temple Bar). Defoe
was fined and pilloried in 1703 at
Charing Cross for his publication of
a satirical pamphlet that attacked the
suppression of non-conformity. The
pillory was covered in flowers by a
crowd which also drank to Defoe's
health. The pillory was abolished for
all offences except perjury in 1815.
It was last used in London in 1830
(set up in Old Bailey for James Bossy,
convicted of perjury) and officially
abolished in England a few years
later.

53 *(right)*

**Convicts sentenced to
transportation, leaving the Sessions
House in Old Bailey**

From 1597, those convicted of
capital crimes could be transported
from the realm. Transportation was
seen as a convenient way of ridding
England of wrongdoers. Perhaps
40,000 convicts were sent to the
West Indies, Virginia, Maryland and
the other North American colonies
(and put to hard labour on the
plantations). After the American
Revolution, the courts sent convicts
to the hulks moored in the Thames
(illustration 222). From 1787 to
1868, about 168,000 convicts were
transported to Australia.

that were erected for each execution. Hangmen were appointed by the Sheriffs of the City of London. A permanent gallows was built in 1571. The gallows was a three-legged construction (seen in illustration 55) known as 'Tyburn Tree', upon which up to 24 people could be hanged at the same time. It was demolished in 1759 and replaced by the turnpike gates and moving gallows. There is only space to mention a few of the victims of Tyburn, some famous, some not. William Wallace was executed there in 1305, and Perkin Warbeck in 1499. In 1534, Elizabeth Barton, the 'Holy Maid of Kent', was executed at Tyburn after making an unwise prophecy – that if Henry VIII married another woman, he would not be King a month later. In 1535, John Houghton, Prior of Charterhouse, refused to take the oath recognising Henry VIII as Supreme Head of the Church in England (rather than the Pope). Houghton (and two other Carthusian priors) were sent to the Tower, then tried at Westminster Hall and condemned to death. They were dragged to Tyburn on hurdles, hanged and then (while still alive), cut down, quartered and disembowelled. Three of the monks of Charterhouse suffered the same fate a few weeks later. Margaret Ward was hung and quartered at Tyburn in 1588 for assisting the escape of a priest, William Watson, from Bridewell. Oliver Plunket, Roman Catholic Archbishop of Armagh, was executed in 1681 for treason. The highwayman Jack Sheppard was executed at Tyburn in 1724 and Jonathan Wild (the Thief-Taker General) in 1725. Robert Tilling was executed in 1760 for murdering his master. The most bizarre hanging took place in 1660. The body of Oliver Cromwell (who died in 1658) was disinterred in 1660, dragged to Tyburn and hanged, then beheaded (the head was displayed at Westminster Hall).

54

Extract from John Rocque's map of the cities of London and Westminster, 1746, showing the place of execution at Tyburn

Tyburn was the most famous place of execution in England, the first recorded being in 1196. The site was close to where Marble Arch now stands. This part of Rocque's map shows the site of Tyburn or Tiburn, near the junction of Tiburn Lane (now Park Lane) and also shows Tiburn Road (now Oxford Street) heading back east towards Newgate Gaol. Just to the south of the gallows is the place 'where soldiers are shot', for example for desertion. In the early days, offenders were hung at Tyburn from trees or from gallows

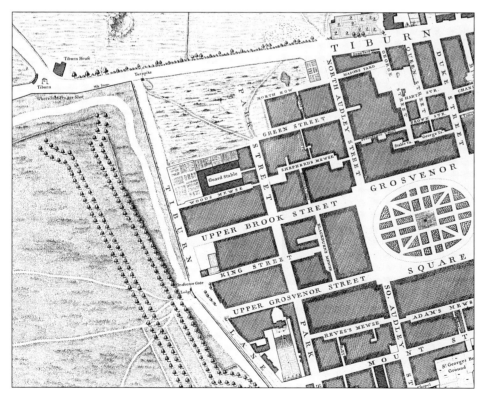

55

The idle apprentice about to be hung at Tyburn

The public hangings at Tyburn were loud and noisy events that might attract thousands of people, in part because hanging days were made public holidays. The condemned were placed in a cart at Newgate Gaol, perhaps given a drink at a tavern opposite and then, to the tolling of the bells of St Sepulchre, taken through the London crowds along Holborn and present-day Oxford Street to the place of execution. The carts sometimes stopped at St Giles-in-the-Fields so that the condemned could have a last drink at a tavern. In Hogarth's series of engravings entitled 'Industry and Idleness', the idle apprentice (Tom Idle) meets his fate at Tyburn. He can be seen in the cart to the left of centre, with his own coffin and a preacher exhorting him to repent (although it was usual for three prisoners to be carried in a cart). In the coach, in front of Tom, can be seen the chaplain (or 'Ordinary') of Newgate. The hangman is lounging on the top of that coach. The rope is being strung over the 'triple tree' and the hangman's assistant awaits, casually sitting on top and smoking his pipe. On the right of the picture can be seen a grandstand, which was known as 'Mother Proctor's Pews', the seats being sold to those who desired a better view of the proceedings. Prisoners originally climbed a ladder with the noose around their neck, then jumped (or were pushed). In the 18th century, the condemned remained in the cart while the noose was attached, then the cart pulled away. Friends or relatives might grab and pull on the legs of the condemned to speed up their death and shorten their suffering. Enormous crowds attended and attracted traders, ruffians, pickpockets and drunkards. In Hogarth's engraving, vendors sell their wares; a fight has broken out and a woman is already selling a sheet entitled the 'last dying speech confession of Tho. Idle'. The riotous behaviour and large crowds at Tyburn resulted in the authorities moving executions to Newgate. The last execution at Tyburn, that of John Austin, took place in 1783. It is estimated that at least 50,000 people swung at Tyburn.

rather than an axe. Large crowds gathered in and around Old Bailey for the executions and nearby rooms with a view of the scaffold could be rented by the wealthy. About 100,000 people were said to have attended the demise of Henry Fauntleroy. About 50,000 gathered in 1864 for the execution of Franz Muller, who committed a murder on a train. A panic arose in a crowd of 40,000 at an execution in 1807: 28 people were trampled to death or suffocated. The last victim outside Newgate was on 26 May 1868. Michael Barrett, a Fenian, was executed for his part in the explosion at Clerkenwell House of Detention (see illustration 215). Executions then took place inside Newgate (see illustrations 186 and 188), with a tolling bell and a black flag flying over the gaol, or at other prisons, such as Pentonville and Wandsworth.

56 *(top right)*
A public execution at the door of Newgate Gaol in about 1809
From 1783, public hangings took place outside Newgate Gaol rather than at Tyburn. The first was on 9 December 1783, when 10 malefactors were hanged by Edward Dennis. Instead of the tree, Newgate had a platform with a 'drop', as shown in this engraving, based on a print published in 1809. Twenty people could be hanged at the same time. Noteworthy victims of this scaffold included Henry Fauntleroy, a banker, who was executed in 1824 for forgery. Some prisoners were killed by other methods. Arthur Thistlewood and four of the other Cato Street conspirators, convicted of treason, were beheaded outside Newgate in 1820. They were first hanged then, when dead, they were beheaded with a surgeon's knife,

57 *(right)*
William Calcraft (1800-1879)
Calcraft was a cobbler who became the best known of the Victorian hangmen. He performed the last public execution outside Newgate (of Michael Barrett) on 26 May 1868. His career at Newgate started when he was paid to flog juvenile offenders. He was appointed hangman in 1829 and served for 45 years. He was reputed to be a kindly man who was fond of children and animals. He was also said, by some, to be a very inefficient hangman; his efforts being little better than strangulation. Other hangmen of Tyburn and Newgate are also interesting. John Price was himself hanged for having raped a woman and Edward Dennis was sentenced to death for taking part in the Gordon Riots (he was reprieved and proceeded to hang other rioters).

VI THE LONDON POLICE

From medieval times, London relied on its equivalent to the parish constable and watchmen (who later became known as 'Charleys') to guard citizens and property from crime. This system was wholly inadequate. Corruption involving the officers of law and order was commonplace and the problems were compounded by the rise of the reward system in the early 18th century. Jonathan Wild, the Thief-Taker General, controlled gangs of thieves and burglars, whilst pocketing the reward money for returning some of the loot that his gangs obtained. Henry Fielding, a Magistrate at Bow Street, and Sir John Fielding, his half-brother, instigated reforms to the system of fighting crime. Their 'thief-takers' and foot patrols became known as the 'Bow Street Runners' and were the model for the Day Police formed in the City in 1784 and the Metropolitan and City Police forces established in London in the early 19th century. The Thames Police force was established in 1798 at 259 Wapping New Stairs to fight the enormous amount of theft of cargoes from ships, smuggling and other crime on the river.

Sir Robert Peel was responsible for the foundation of the Metropolitan Police in 1829, so they became known as 'Peelers' or 'Bobbies'. There were originally 10 Police offices including Bow Street, Marlborough Street, Hatton Garden, Worship Street, Whitechapel, Shadwell and 4 Whitehall Place (Scotland Yard). The Thames Police Force and the Bow Street Runners were merged into the Metropolitan Police in 1839. In 1830, the force consisted of about 3,300 officers but it had grown to almost 16,000 officers by 1900 and over 28,000 by 1989, with almost 200 police stations. A Detective Branch was established in 1842, although it had only 15 officers by 1868. The Special Irish Branch was established in 1885, in response to a bombing campaign by the Fenians, and was later renamed Special Branch.

The City of London Police Force was established in 1839 with jurisdiction over the Square Mile. The headquarters are at 26 Old Jewry, with divisions now based at Snow Hill and Bishopsgate, and the mounted branch based at Wood Street.

58
A group of Metropolitan Police officers, *c.*1900

59
Mounted officers of the City of London Police Force
This photograph shows mounted officers, c. 1902 near King Street. The crest of the City of London can be seen on their helmets. Their horses were kept at the Whitbread Brewery stables and later with the Lord Mayor's coach horses until 1964, when stables were built at Wood Street Police Station.

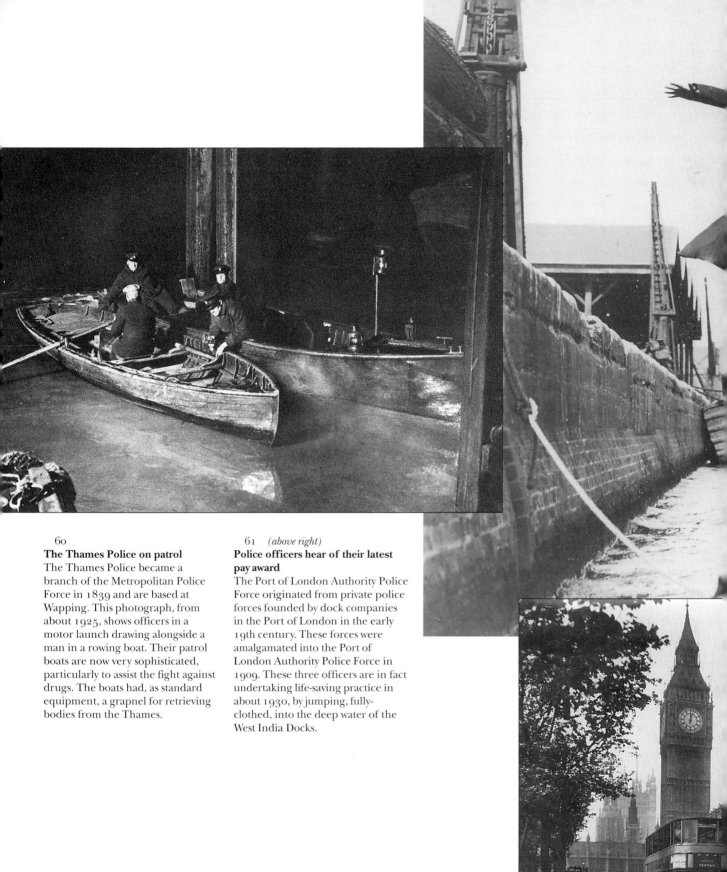

60

The Thames Police on patrol

The Thames Police became a branch of the Metropolitan Police Force in 1839 and are based at Wapping. This photograph, from about 1925, shows officers in a motor launch drawing alongside a man in a rowing boat. Their patrol boats are now very sophisticated, particularly to assist the fight against drugs. The boats had, as standard equipment, a grapnel for retrieving bodies from the Thames.

61 *(above right)*

Police officers hear of their latest pay award

The Port of London Authority Police Force originated from private police forces founded by dock companies in the Port of London in the early 19th century. These forces were amalgamated into the Port of London Authority Police Force in 1909. These three officers are in fact undertaking life-saving practice in about 1930, by jumping, fully-clothed, into the deep water of the West India Docks.

62 *(below left)*
Scotland Yard from the Embankment
An office of the Metropolitan Police Force was established in 1829 in 4 Whitehall Place, Westminster. This was one of a row of houses built over two alleys that had been named Middle Scotland Yard and Little Scotland Yard. This became the headquarters of the Metropolitan Police. The building was badly damaged by a Fenian bomb in 1884 and the headquarters moved in 1891 to a new building, close to Westminster Bridge. This building, designed by Norman Shaw, was named Scotland House, but known as New Scotland Yard. It was faced with granite quarried by convicts at Dartmoor. This photograph dates from about 1920. The Metropolitan Police headquarters moved to a new building on Victoria Street in 1967. The old headquarters was then renamed as the Norman Shaw Building and used as offices by Members of Parliament.

63 *(below)*
Wood Green Police Station: a typical suburban London Police station
Some police stations were, or looked like, suburban houses.

64

The Police Station in Hyde Park
Some police stations were much more attractive. The station in Hyde Park is shown here in a very attractive setting but the park has not always been considered so delightful. Highwaymen plagued Hyde Park in the late 17th and early 18th centuries and the park was also a popular venue for duels.

65

The cells at Bishopsgate Police Station in 1939

66

A watch house to deter the body snatchers
Until the Anatomy Act of 1832, only the corpses of murderers were legally available for dissection and study by the medical profession. The demand for bodies outstripped supply and so high prices were offered and obtained for these essential study-aids. This persuaded some to pay nocturnal visits to graveyards and disinter fresh corpses and this in turn led to the construction of watch houses (also used by watchmen and constables). This house was built at Rotherhithe in 1824.

VII TEMPLE BAR AND THE INNS OF COURT

Temple Bar stood where Fleet Street became the Strand and marked the western boundary of the City of London. Originally, there was only a chain that could be pulled across the road. A timber gate, of the 14th or 15th century, escaped the Great Fire but it was replaced by a new Bar, designed by Wren, which was completed in 1672. Temple Bar was removed in 1878 because it was so narrow that it caused traffic congestion (and was too narrow for the planned widening of the Strand). It lay in pieces in a yard in Farringdon Street for many years but was then rebuilt in Theobald's Park in Hertfordshire. There are plans for its return to London. A monument with a dragon was placed at the site in 1880. The heads of executed traitors were sometimes displayed on spikes on Temple Bar from the late 17th century. Sometimes other parts of the traitors' bodies were also displayed. The first occasion appears to have been in 1684, when parts of the body of Sir Thomas Armstrong were displayed (having been boiled in salt so that birds would not eat them). Some heads of Jacobites were displayed in 1746, after Bonnie Prince Charlie's failure to take the throne. The heads of two of the rebels could still be seen on Temple Bar as late as 1760. The last one was blown down in 1772.

The Inns of Court have for centuries had the exclusive right to call students to the Bar to act as advocates in the Royal Courts of England and Wales (this right is only now diminishing as solicitor advocates obtain rights of audience before the higher courts). The four Inns of Court – Middle Temple, Inner Temple, Lincoln's Inn and Gray's Inn – are independent, self-governing bodies (subject only to the Senate of the Inns of Court, which deals with certain aspects of professional practice, discipline and education). They are each styled an 'Honourable Society' and governed by Benchers. The references to 'Inn' probably derive from the town houses or mansions, used as hostels for barristers and students, in which the Inns of Court were born. Oxford and Cambridge Universities did not instruct students until the 18th century on the English Common Law and so students would attend in London, near to the courts at Westminster, to study. Barristers also needed lodgings in London so as to attend the courts in term time (and the students needed practising barristers to conduct lectures and moots) and so the Inns were born. In Elizabethan times, legal education at the Inns could extend over seven or eight years, but is now very much shorter (since most legal education is provided by universities). The Bar (and membership of the Inns of Court) was very much smaller before this century. In 1779, there were only 218 barristers (compared with over 7,000 today). Attorneys and solicitors could also once be members of the Inns of Court, but they were gradually excluded.

The area of the Temple was acquired in the 12th century by the Knights Templar, a religious order of knights, formed to protect pilgrims travelling to Jerusalem. The property was soon known by their name. The order became rich and powerful. In 1162, the Pope rendered the Order immune from all jurisdictions other than that of the Holy See. The monarchs of Western Europe were jealous and anxious of the Order's power (and coveted the Order's riches). The Templars were therefore suppressed in 1312, accused of heresy. Some of their English property passed to another order – the Knights Hospitaller. Within a few years, lawyers (the predecessors of the Societies of Inner and Middle Temple) had taken leases of parts of the Temple. In 1326, one body of lawyers leased certain houses and, in 1356, another body leased a hall, some chambers, a garden and a stable. The first mention of a society known as Middle Temple occurs in a will dated 1404. The Hospitallers were suppressed in 1539 and in 1609, James I granted the Temple to the two Societies of Inner and Middle Temple. Noteworthy members or students of Middle Temple include Sir Francis Drake, the Duke of Monmouth, Sir William Blackstone and Lord Scarman. Noteworthy members of Inner Temple include Sir Edward Coke, the first Lord Chief Justice of England and later Attorney-General, Thomas Wentworth, Earl of Strafford, Lord Chief Justice Jeffreys (who had, as a barrister, chambers in Hare Court) and Lord Chancellor Harcourt (after whom Harcourt Buildings are named).

Despite much research, the origin of Lincoln's Inn, which was founded in the mid-14th century, remains uncertain. The traditional view was that Lincoln's Inn derived its name from Henry de Lacy, Earl of Lincoln (died 1311), that he brought together a society of lawyers and that the Inn was built on the site of his palace. The Inn has used his coat of arms for over three centuries and they appear on a gateway built in the early 16th century. Henry de Lacy was a Justice and minister of King Edward I and may have been closely involved in the legal reforms of the late 13th century by which clerics were displaced as lawyers by laymen. However, Henry de Lacy's palace was at the north end of Shoe Lane, near St Andrew, Holborn. Furthermore, most of the site of Lincoln's Inn on the west side of Chancellor's (now Chancery) Lane – the Old Hall, chapel, gatehouse and Old Square – was the London residence of the Bishops of Chichester from 1227 until 1413. The property was rented by the Society of Lincoln's Inn from the Bishop of Chichester between 1415 and 1422 (the year in which the 'Black Books' – the records of the Inn – commence). The Inn purchased the freehold of the property in 1580. However, it is possible that the Society was there much earlier. Much legal business may have been undertaken in Henry de Lacy's house. A society of lawyers may have been born in his house, or nearby. Even if Henry de Lacy had no direct hand in the formation of the Inn, the early members of the society of lawyers (which became the Honourable Society of Lincoln's Inn) may have named their society after him.

The Society of Lincoln's Inn consists of Masters of the Bench, Utter Barristers and clerks or students. Lincoln's Inn is particularly renowned for producing equity lawyers who practised in the Court of Chancery. Famous members or students of Lincoln's Inn included Sir John Fortescue, Chief Justice of the King's Bench in 1442, Sir Thomas More (admitted to the Inn in 1496), Sir Mathew Hale (another Chief Justice of the King's Bench), Lords Mansfield, Eldon, Selborne, Hailsham and Denning. There were many who made their mark outside the law; Oliver Cromwell, Walpole, William Pitt the Younger, Lord Macaulay, Disraeli, Gladstone (see illustration 17), H.H. Asquith (see illustration 163), David Garrick and Charles Kingsley. As noted, the Inn's records, the 'Black Books', date back to 1422. Sir Robert Megarry noted (*see* bibliography) that the 'Black Books' include a decree of 1489 by the Benchers of Lincoln's Inn to the effect that any member of the Inn who fornicated with a woman in his chambers should be fined 100 shillings. However, if 'he shall have her or enjoy her' in the gardens or in Chancellor's Lane, the fine would be only 20 shillings. I do not know whether this decree is still in force.

Gray's Inn is on the site of the manor of Portpool in Holborn, which was obtained in 1294 by Reginald de Gray, Chief Justice of Chester. He probably housed students of law at the premises and Gray's Inn may therefore be the oldest of the Inns. Gray's family owned the Inn until 1506. In Rocque's map, the Inn can be clearly seen between Holborn and Gray's Inn Lane (now Road). To the south end is Holbourn Court (now South Square). North of that is Coney Court which, in 1793, was merged with Chapel Court and renamed Gray's Inn Square. Famous members of Gray's Inn include Thomas Cromwell, Sir Thomas Gresham, Sir William Cecil (later Lord Burghley), Sir Francis Bacon and Lord Birkenhead (see illustration 150).

67 (right)
Temple Bar on the Strand, c.1829
This engraving of Temple Bar, from a drawing by Thomas Shepherd, was published in 1829.

68 (below)
Temple Bar in 1878
This photograph was taken from the west shortly before Temple Bar was removed from London. On the left, buildings are being demolished to make way for the new Royal Courts of Justice. The room over the arch was once used by Child's Bank, which stood on the Fleet Street side of Temple Bar.

69 (below right)
Temple Bar in Theobald's Park, Hertfordshire
This photograph shows Temple Bar in retirement. Plans have often been made for its return to London.

70

The new marker of the boundary of the City of London; the dragon of Fleet Street

The new boundary marker between the Cities of London and Westminster, on the site of Temple Bar, is a stone pillar surmounted by a winged dragon, popularly (but incorrectly) called a griffin. This view, from about 1910, looks to the east.

71-74
Tokens of the four Inns of Court
Each of the Inns of Court has a token or badge, based upon their coats of arms. The Inner Temple has a Pegasus (a winged horse) said to have been adopted in 1563. The token of Middle Temple, the 'Agnus Dei', was first used by it in the early 17th century. The token of Gray's Inn is a griffin, also adopted in the 17th century. The token of Lincoln's Inn, consisting of a lion and a mill-rind (the fastening in a millstone) has been used since 1516.

75

A view of Temple and the Thames in 1720

This view of the Temple in about 1720, reproduced from *The history of the Temple, London* by J.B. Williamson (1924), shows how little the Temple has changed since that time. One exception is that the Thames used to pass right by the Inns; note the Temple Stairs (stairs and a small pier) to the left of the view, from which the lawyers could take boats to the courts at Westminster. In 1441, Eleanor Cobham, Duchess of Gloucester was accused of witchcraft against Henry VI. She was ordered to do penance; to walk (clad in a white sheet and carrying a taper) to St Paul's Cathedral. She landed at Temple Stairs before walking up Fleet Street, and then to St Paul's Cathedral. Temple Stairs were demolished in 1865 as Embankment was built between Temple and the Thames. Much of the Temple was destroyed in the Great Fire, including the whole of King's Bench Walk. There were later fires in the Temple; much of King's Bench Walk burned again in 1677, part of Temple Church was burned in 1679 and half of Brick Court was destroyed in 1704. The Temple was badly damaged in the bombing of 1940 and 1941 – Temple Church, Middle Temple Hall, Temple Cloisters and many other parts were destroyed or badly damaged. However, many of the damaged buildings have been rebuilt or restored and so the Temple is again a glorious place to visit or work in.

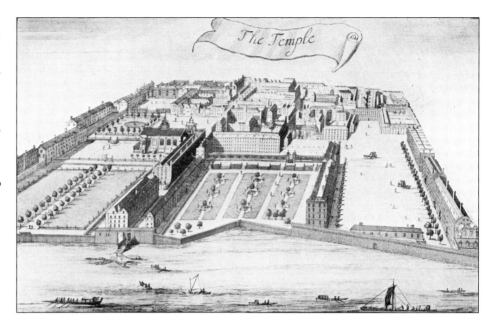

76

Prince Henry's Room, number 17, Fleet Street and the gate to Inner Temple

In 1610, the chambers over the gateway to Inner Temple on Fleet Street were sold to William Blake. His tavern to the east, the *Prince's Arms*, was then extended over the gateway. From 1795 to 1816, the premises were used as a tavern and as a waxworks. Any connection with Henry, Prince of Wales (the eldest son of James I) is dubious and primarily based upon the Prince of Wales' feathers and initials 'PH' appearing in the Jacobean plaster ceiling. London County Council acquired the premises in 1900 and 'Prince Henry's Room' is open to the public.

77-79

Three views of Temple Church: in about 1828, in 1904 and in 1945
The two Societies of Middle and Inner Temple have always shared Temple Church. The Norman Round Church was built by the Knights Templar and consecrated in 1185. They added a chancel in about 1240. Their Order was dissolved in 1312 but the church contains eight effigies of 12th- and 13th-century crusader knights, including the 3rd and 4th Earls of Pembroke. The authorities differ as to whether any of the effigies are Templars. Temple Church was restored in 1681-3 and in 1828. The earliest of these three views (illustration 77) is an engraving from a drawing by Thomas Shepherd, showing the church after its restoration of 1828. The conical roof to the Round was added in 1841-3. The postcard at illustration 78 is from a photograph by Taunt & Co, showing the conical roof of the church, the Temple Cloisters on the far left (destroyed during the war, but rebuilt) and Lamb Building on the right (see illustration 92), also now destroyed. The church was badly damaged by incendiary bombs during air raids in 1941 and the postcard at illustration 79, from 1944 or 1945, shows the damage. The card is marked as 'passed by the censor'. Temple Church has now been restored.

80 *(below)*
The porch of Temple Church

81 *(bottom)*
The door of Temple Church

82 *(right)*
The tomb of Edmund Plowden (1518-84) in Temple Church
Edmund Plowden studied at Cambridge then entered Middle Temple and was called to the Bar. He published many works on the law and was a Member of Parliament in the reign of Queen Mary. As a Catholic, he was barred from most public offices following the accession of Elizabeth. Plowden was Treasurer of Middle Temple during the rebuilding of Middle Temple Hall. His monument survived WW2 (by being bricked up).

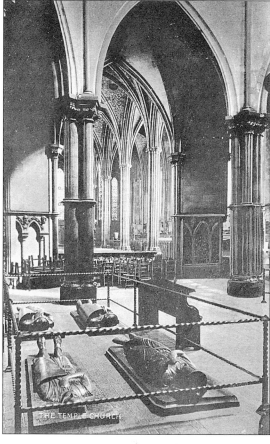

83-85
Three views of the interior of Temple Church
Illustrations 83 and 84 are an engraving and a postcard showing the interior of the Round Church with the effigies of knights on the floor. Illustration 85 is a postcard showing the pulpit and chancel, looking west.

86 *(left)*
Middle Temple Lane
It is still a joy to walk up or down the cobbles of Middle Temple Lane, which leads down from Fleet Street towards Embankment (previously to Temple Stairs). Hare Court is on the right. This photograph was taken by 'A.R.W.', that is Mr. Arthur Witts, a wig-maker (see illustration 87) in about 1920.

87 *(below)*
The wig shop of Arthur Witts in Middle Temple Lane
Arthur Witts was one of the makers of wigs in the Temple. His shop was at the Fleet Street end of Middle Temple Lane (another wig shop was located in Temple Cloisters). However, he was also a photographer, who sold postcards and guidebooks, as well as wigs. Samples of all his wares can be seen stacked in the shop window. This view dates from about 1926. Mr. Witts' sign noted his '30 years with Ede & Ravenscroft', who still supply wigs to the profession.

88 *(above)*
The interior of Middle Temple Hall, looking east
The original Middle Temple Hall, dating from about 1320, was replaced by a new hall in 1572/3, under the direction of Edmund Plowden (see illustration 82), the Treasurer of the Inn. It has perhaps the finest Elizabethan roof in London. The walls of the Hall were badly damaged in WW2, but the ceiling survived and the Hall has been restored. The diary of John Manningham, a barrister, for 2 February 1602/3, notes that the play, *Twelfth Night*, was performed in the Hall that evening. He did not record the presence of Elizabeth I or Shakespeare. Later suggestions that they were present therefore seem unlikely to be true.

89 *(below)*
The gardens and Hall of Middle Temple

HALL AND GARDENS, MIDDLE TEMPLE, BUILT 1572.

90 *(left)*

**The memorial to Oliver Goldsmith
in the Temple graveyard**
Goldsmith (1728-74), poet,
playwright and novelist, was not a
member of either Middle or Inner
Temple, but he had chambers in
2 Brick Court. He died with debts of
almost £2,000 and was buried in the
north churchyard of the Temple.
The exact site of his grave is now lost
but a memorial to him remains; the

plain stone to the bottom left of this postcard (merely stating 'Here lies Oliver Goldsmith'), not the more interesting tomb in the centre. There are many other important memorials in Temple Church or graveyard, including that to Sir Nicholas Hare, the Master of the Rolls during the reign of Queen Mary, after whom Hare Court in the Temple is named.

91 *(left)*
The gardens between Inner and Middle Temple
This view of Inner Temple Gardens was taken from Fountain Court. It was in these gardens that Shakespeare set his famous scene in *Henry VI, part I* of the plucking of the red and white roses of the Houses of Lancaster and York. The turreted building on the right is the old library of Middle Temple (see illustration 94).

92 *(right)*
Lamb Building, Temple
Lamb Building, so-called because of the lamb (the 'Agnus Dei') that can be seen over the entrance in this photograph, was part of Inner Temple, standing to the south of Temple Church. Inner Temple sold the building to Middle Temple after the Great Fire of 1666. It was destroyed in 1941. The Inns decided not to rebuild on the south side of the church and so a new Lamb Building was built to the west of Elm Court.

93
Pump Court, Temple
Another photograph by Mr. Witts the wig-maker. This shows Pump Court (before the destruction during WW2), from the arcade on the east side, looking towards the arch that leads to Middle Temple Lane. In the white winter of 1679, a great fire in the Temple destroyed Pump Court. Attempts were made to quench the fire with beer from the cellars of Inner Temple, the only unfrozen liquid available.

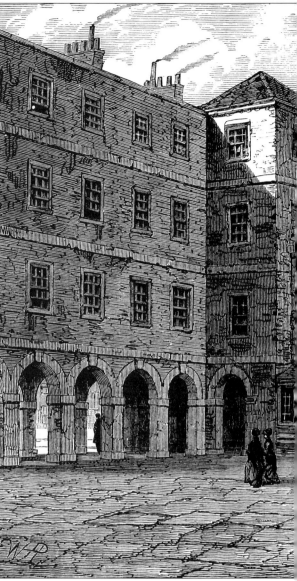

94 *(above left)*
The Library of Middle Temple
This Library was built in Middle Temple Gardens in 1861 but destroyed by bombing in 1941. A new library was built in 1956.

95 *(left)*
The Temple Fountain in Fountain Court
This drawing, from *Old and New London*, is based upon a painting and engraving of about 1735. The Court was laid out, and the foundations of the fountain dug, in 1681. The fountain jet rose as high as 30 feet. Middle Temple Hall is on the right.

97　*(below)*

The Hall and Library of Inner Temple
The medieval Hall of Inner Temple and the Library were replaced in 1869 by a new Hall (on the left of this photograph) and Library (on the right). These buildings were almost completely destroyed in WW2 but rebuilt in the 1950s. Inner Temple Library now contains about 100,000 books but the members of Inner Temple have not always concentrated on their studies. The relative importance of books and victuals in earlier times is illustrated by the fact that, in 1506, Inner Temple Library consisted of only a few books and there was no librarian – care of the books was one of the subsidiary duties of Inner Temple's chief butler.

96　*(above)*

Part of Inner Temple in 1800
This drawing, from *Old and New London*, is based upon a painting of about 1800. Temple Cloisters are on the left. The upper part of Temple Church can be seen on the right, standing behind shops that sold wigs, boots, shoes and even music. These were demolished around 1820.

98-99
Two views of the interior of Inner Temple Hall
These postcards show the Hall at the start of the 20th century.

100
The Inner Temple

101
King's Bench Walk, Inner Temple
This view is towards the south and Thames Embankment. King's Bench Walk took its name from the King's Bench Office (that is the court office) located there until it was burnt down in 1677. Most of King's Bench Walk had also been burned in 1666, but was rebuilt.

102-103   *(above)*
The gateway from Chancery Lane into Lincoln's Inn
These two views are of the beautiful red brick gateway into Lincoln's Inn from the Chancery Lane side. Illustration 102 shows the gateway in the 19th century. Illustration 103 is a postcard from about 1920. The gateway was built between 1518 and 1521 by Sir Thomas Lovell. The coats of arms above it are Lovell's and those of Henry VIII and Henry de Lacy. The display of de Lacy's arms supports the view that he founded the Inn, or at least that it was thought (when the gate was built) that he had done so.

104   *(below left)*
Old Buildings, Lincoln's Inn and the gateway from Chancery Lane
This view shows the same gateway, but from inside Lincoln's Inn. Old Buildings were built between 1490 and 1520 and originally known as Gatehouse Court.

105   *(above right)*
The Old Hall and Chapel of Lincoln's Inn
This engraving, from a drawing by Thomas Shepherd, was published in 1830. At the left is the Old Hall of Lincoln's Inn, which dates from 1492 (and replaced an earlier hall, demolished in 1489). To the right is the Chapel, which was consecrated in 1623 (replacing an older chapel of the Bishop of Chichester). The archways to the undercroft (see illustration 113) can be seen at the base of the Chapel. Since 1830, four small towers or spires have been added to each side of the Chapel's roof.

106 *(below)*

The Old Hall, Lincoln's Inn
This postcard shows the Old Hall, which was completed in 1492 and later enlarged (1623-4). It was the venue, out of term time, for the sitting of the Lord Chancellor's Court of Chancery from 1734 until the opening of the Royal Courts of Justice in 1882 (see illustration 45). It was the setting for much of the case of 'Jarndyce v. Jarndyce' in *Bleak House* by Charles Dickens. The Old Hall was small and so a new hall was built (see illustrations 107-8) but the Old Hall was also rebuilt 1926-8.

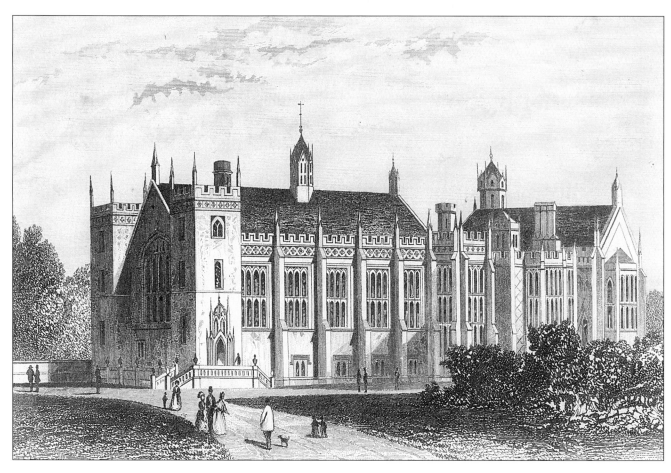

107
The New Hall and Library, Lincoln's Inn
The New Hall and Library were opened in 1845. The old Library had been built in 1505.

108
The New Hall, Lincoln's Inn
This view, from about 1900, shows the New Hall from Lincoln's Inn Fields. To the extreme left is the western end of the Library.

109
The Library, Lincoln's Inn
This view, again taken from Lincoln's Inn Fields in about 1900, shows the western end of the Library of Lincoln's Inn in more detail.

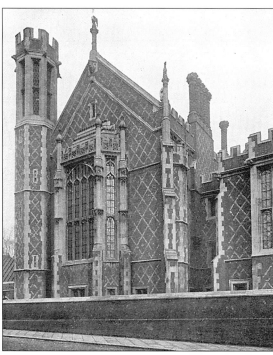

110
The interior of the Hall of Lincoln's Inn
This view is towards the northern end of the Hall. Along the walls to either side there are painted the coats of arms of distinguished members of Lincoln's Inn.

111
The interior of the Library, Lincoln's Inn
This is one of the most beautiful libraries in the world. The light and the galleries of wonderful books are breathtaking. It holds over 80,000 books and is also one of the oldest collections in the world.

LONDON ENTRANCE TO LINCOLNS INN FROM THE "FIELDS".
THE LIBRARY ON THE LEFT IS ONE OF THE OLDEST & MOST VALUABLE IN THE WORLD.

Copyright

112 *(above)*

The entrance to Lincoln's Inn from Lincoln's Inn Fields

This is the West Gate, built in 1845. Lincoln's Inn Fields were occasionally used for executions. The Catholic Anthony Babington was implicated in plots in favour of Mary Queen of Scots in 1586. He had been found in Lincoln's Inn Fields with a wax figure of Queen Elizabeth, pierced with pins, allegedly attempting to contrive her death by witchcraft. He was hanged for a few moments then cut down and cut in pieces 'with due precaution for the protraction of pain'. Thirteen other conspirators were also executed here. In 1683, Lord William Russell was beheaded here for alleged complicity in the Rye House Plot.

113 *(above left)*

The open undercroft of the Chapel of Lincoln's Inn

Members of Lincoln's Inn originally used the chapels of Our Lady and St Richard that had been part of the Bishop of Chichester's Palace. A new Chapel was built (1620-23). The open undercroft was intended as a place for barristers or students to walk and talk, but it was also used for burials, including those of John Thurloe, Cromwell's Secretary of State (died 1668) and Sir John Anstruther, Chief Justice of Bengal (died 1811).

114　(far left)
The interior of Lincoln's Inn Chapel

115　(top)
Stone Buildings, Lincoln's Inn
This photograph shows Stone Buildings in about 1900, the major part having been built in 1775 and 1780. The Inns of Court Regiment has its headquarters at 10 Stone Buildings.

116　(above)
Wildy's Bookshop in the south entrance to New Square, Lincoln's Inn
This view, taken from New Square, shows the entrance from Carey Street into the square at its south-east corner. The entrance was built in 1693 and known as Back Gate. Wildy & Sons is a goldmine for all collectors of books, prints and ephemera concerning the law. The shop was established in the rooms either side of the gateway in 1830. For many years, Wildy's also had another shop in the cloisters in Middle Temple (the shop was destroyed by bombing in 1941).

117 *(right)*
Gray's Inn Hall, Chapel and Library
This engraving, from a drawing by
Thomas Shepherd, is from the early
19th century. The library was built
in the 16th century, but was reduced
to ruins (with the Hall and Chapel)
on the night of 10-11 May 1941. The
reconstructed library was opened in
1958.

118 *(above)*
**The interior of the Hall of Gray's
Inn**
The Hall was built around 1555-60
(replacing an earlier hall). It was
destroyed in 1941, but rebuilt. The
first performance of Shakespeare's
Comedy of Errors was in this Hall in
December 1594.

119 *(right)*
The interior of Gray's Inn Chapel
There was a chapel at Gray's Inn
from as early as 1315, but major
reconstruction took place in the
17th century and in 1893. The
Chapel was also destroyed in 1941
but rebuilt.

120
The gardens of Gray's Inn in 1770
The gardens were laid out by Sir Francis Bacon in the early 17th century and became a popular place for walks by members of fashionable society.

121
The statue of Sir Francis Bacon, Gray's Inn
Francis Bacon was admitted to Gray's Inn in 1576, called to the Bar in 1582 and became a Bencher in 1586. He was later Treasurer of Gray's Inn and responsible for laying out Gray's Inn Gardens. Bacon was a Member of Parliament 1584-1620 and knighted by James I. He wrote a large number of legal, literary and philosophical works. He was appointed Solicitor-General in 1607 and Attorney-General in 1613. In 1618, he was appointed as Lord Chancellor and created Baron Verulam. He was made Viscount St Alban in 1621 but then came before the House of Lords charged with bribery. He confessed to being guilty of corruption. He was prohibited from sitting in Parliament and fined, but his confinement in the Tower only lasted a few days. His statue was unveiled in South Square in 1912. The statue survived the Blitz, although it was damaged.

VIII SERJEANTS' INN AND THE INNS OF CHANCERY

Serjeants-at-Law are first recorded in the late 13th century and were members of the Order of the Coif. The coif was a white silk cap that Serjeants wore in court until wigs came into fashion for advocates in the reign of Charles II. Serjeants were senior advocates who were promoted from the ranks of barristers. They were summoned by writ under the Great Seal to leave their Inns to join the society of Serjeants. Membership conferred the exclusive right of audience in the Court of Common Pleas (until 1846). Furthermore, until the Judicature Act 1873, it was only from the rank of Serjeants (usually about 40 of them) that Common Law judges (that is of the Courts of King's Bench and Common Pleas) could be appointed. By the 19th century, this meant merely that a barrister who was to be appointed as a Judge, but who was not a Serjeant-at-Law, was immediately appointed as one. Following the abolition of their exclusive rights, the Serjeants dissolved their Society (in 1876) and returned to their Inns of Court.

Little is known of the origins of the Inns of Chancery. It is also uncertain why they were called Inns of 'Chancery', although it may be that in medieval times, they trained Clerks of Chancery (that is the government department, not the Court), who were responsible for preparing writs that were issued from the Common Law courts. Each Inn was styled an 'Honourable Society' and consisted of a Principal (equivalent to the Treasurer of an Inn of Court), Ancients (the equivalent of Benchers) and Juniors (the other members). The Inns of Chancery can be considered as junior or preparatory Inns. Their members – attorneys, clerks and students – had no right of audience in the courts. However, whilst some students became attorneys or solicitors, some proceeded to admission at one of the Inns of Court (and were then called to the Bar). Indeed, until the early 17th century, it was usually a pre-condition of entry to the Inns of Court that a student had been a member of an Inn of Chancery for a year or two. Each Inn of Chancery was subordinate to an Inn of Court that provided a 'Reader' to give lectures to its students and conduct moots. The Inns of Chancery did not have chapels, but their members used nearby churches. The Inns gradually lost their importance for education because students tended to enrol directly in one of the Inns of Court if they wished to be called to the Bar, and the Law Society (see illustration 139) began to provide for education for attorneys and solicitors. Many rooms in the Inns were used (as early as the 18th century in some cases) as London residences of non-lawyers and the Inns of Chancery then became little more than dining clubs.

Three Inns of Chancery are not illustrated here. St George's Inn was near Old Bailey but ceased to be used in the 15th century, the students migrating to New Inn (see illustration 133). Thavies Inn (or Davy's Inn) was affiliated to Lincoln's Inn and seems to have been an Inn of Chancery from about the time that Lincoln's Inn purchased the freehold of the property in 1549. The property was in Shoe Lane, next to the church of St Andrew's Holborn. Lincoln's Inn refused to grant the Inn a new lease in about 1769 and this led to the dissolution of the Inn. The property was burned down in about 1800. Strand Inn, affiliated to Middle Temple, was situated on the south side of the Strand near the church of St Mary-le-Strand. The property was also known as Chester Inn because it had been owned by the Bishops of Chester. It was destroyed in the 16th century to make way for Protector Somerset's new palace.

122
Serjeants' Inn, Fleet Street
The Serjeants obtained a lease of a site on Fleet Street in about 1425 as a commons (and for lodging during term time). The Serjeants also acquired a site in Chancery Lane (see illustration 123) at about the same time and also used a building known as Scrope's Inn, on Holborn, in the period 1459-96. The hall on Fleet Street was destroyed in the Great Fire of 1666 but was rebuilt. In about 1732, the Serjeants gave up the Fleet Street site but remained in Chancery Lane. The Fleet Street building was almost entirely destroyed during the Blitz. This drawing, from *Old and New London*, is based upon a print published in 1804, showing the Inn as rebuilt after the departure of the Serjeants.

123
Serjeants' Inn Hall, Chancery Lane
The Serjeants acquired a site on the south-east side of Chancery Lane in 1425. The Inn was rebuilt in 1837. The hall was then used for some hearings by the Court of Exchequer. The Chancery Lane building was sold in 1877 and demolished in 1909. This engraving is from a drawing by Thomas Shepherd of the early 19th century, showing the Hall and some of the chambers.

124 (above)

The Hall of Staple Inn

In the 14th century, Staple Inn was a
meeting place for wool merchants.
Lawyers then resided in the Inn and
formed an Inn of Chancery in 1378.
The Inn became affiliated to Gray's
Inn; the Benchers of Gray's Inn
purchasing the freehold of the
Staple Inn property (in trust for the
members of Staple Inn) in 1529. In
Elizabethan times the Inn was
occupied by about 145 law students.
However, by the 18th century the
Inn was declining as a legal school
and many chambers were being used
as offices by attorneys and solicitors.
Many non-lawyers took rooms there,
including Dr. Samuel Johnson in
1759. This engraving, from a
drawing by Thomas Shepherd, was
published in 1830. The Inn was sold
to the Prudential Assurance
Company in 1884 and the Hall is let
to the Institute of Actuaries. The
Hall (built in about 1580) and some
of the chambers of Staple Inn were
destroyed by a flying bomb in 1944
but the Hall was carefully
reconstructed.

LONDON. OLD HOUSES, STAPLE INN, HO

125 (left)
The Holborn frontage of Staple Inn
This is the better known view of
Staple Inn – the Elizabethan-style
frontage on Holborn, with a gateway,
opposite the Gray's Inn Road. This
part of the Inn was built between
1545 and 1588. The Hall and
courtyards of the Inn are behind this
frontage, extending down to
Southampton Buildings.

126 (above)
**The Holborn frontage of Staple Inn,
1804**
The timber and plaster of the
Holborn front of Staple Inn has not
always been visible. In the 17th
century, it was covered by plaster
rendering as shown in this engraving
published in 1804. After purchasing
the Inn in 1884, the Prudential
Assurance Company restored the
façade by stripping off the plaster
rendering to reveal the original
timbers. Although the façade was
reconstructed, the building behind
it was demolished in 1937 and a new
building constructed in its place.

127
The interior of the Hall of Staple Inn
This watercolour was executed in about 1882 by John Crowther.

128
The outer courtyard of Staple Inn

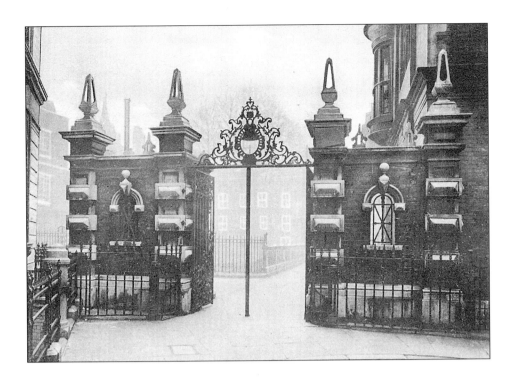

129
**The entrance gates to Staple Inn
from Southampton Buildings**

130
The water garden of Staple Inn
Staple Inn has two courts, between
which is the Hall. The water garden
is in the Inner Court, on the
southern side of the Hall (near to
Southampton buildings).

LONDON. Staple Inn, Holborn. No. 1038.

131 *(left)*

The Hall of Lyon's Inn

Lyon's Inn can be seen on Rocque's map – it was on the north side of the Strand (and south of Wych Street) – just to the east of St Mary-le-Strand. Parts of Bush House and Australia House now occupy the site. The property was originally a tavern with the sign of a lion. Lyon's Inn became an Inn of Chancery in about 1420 and was affiliated to Inner Temple. Lyon's Inn declined in the 17th and 18th centuries and its buildings were demolished in 1863. Most of its records have disappeared. This engraving is from a drawing by Thomas Shepherd.

132 *(below)*

Clement's Inn

Clement's Inn, in the parish of St Clement Danes, was affiliated to the Inner Temple. It was a 'house' of law from the late 15th century. It was on the north side of the Strand, to the west of the site of the Royal Courts of Justice and to the north of the church of St Clement Danes (in which certain pews were reserved for members of the Inn). In 1708, it was described as 'a Hall and many

handsome chambers, built around three courts'. The old Hall was rebuilt in 1715. This print, by Samuel Ireland, was published in 1800. Some of the buildings of the Inn were sold in 1868, to make way for the Royal Courts of Justice. The others were sold in 1884. The Hall was demolished in 1893.

133 *(right)*

New Inn

New Inn is shown on Rocque's map to the north of Wych Street and west of Clement's Inn. The property was originally a common inn or tavern named *Our Lady Inn* which was converted in about 1460 by law students who had migrated from an earlier, but dilapidated, Inn of Chancery near Old Bailey, named St George's Inn. New Inn was affiliated to Middle Temple. Sir Thomas More was a student of the Inn before his admission to Middle Temple. This print, by Samuel Ireland, was published in 1800. Membership declined in the 19th century and the property was compulsorily acquired by London County Council in 1899 for its scheme to build Aldwych and Kingsway.

134
Barnard's Inn

Barnard's Inn was an Inn of Chancery affiliated to Gray's Inn. A building at the site, south of Holborn and close to Fetter Lane, was leased in about 1454 to the Dean (named Macworth) and Chapter of Lincoln. It became known as Macworth's Inn. The Dean and Chapter then leased it to one Lionel Bernard or Barnard, by whose name it then became known. He may have been a lawyer, or even have headed a society of lawyers. It subsequently became an Inn of Chancery. The Hall dates from about 1540. The Principal, Ancients and students of Barnard's Inn used to march in full robes to services at St Andrew's Holborn (illustration 178), where they had their own pews. The Inn produced many good students but, in 1601, a member, Mr. Bellamy, was fined 3s. 4d. for 'striking the cook in the kitchen'. In 1633, Thomas Marsh was so refractory that he was expelled and the doors of his rooms locked. He broke off the locks and so was imprisoned in the Marshalsea. The Inn declined in the 19th century. There were only about forty admissions between 1800 and 1870 and none after that year. The Inn became little more than a dining club. The Dean and Chapter of Lincoln refused to grant a new lease to the Inn and the property was sold in 1892 to the Worshipful Company of Mercers. The company's school occupied the property until 1959. The Hall still stands near the south side of Holborn and is occupied by the Prudential Assurance Company.

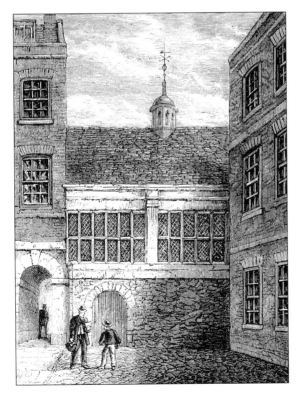

135-136
Two views of Clifford's Inn in the 19th century

Clifford's Inn was on the north side of Fleet Street and can be seen on Rocque's map, behind St Dunstan-in-the-West and Serjeant's Inn, Chancery Lane. It had a frontage on Fetter Lane and a passage and gateway connected the Inn to Fleet Street. Clifford's Inn was named after Robert de Clifford to whom Edward II granted the property in about 1310. The property was leased to law students in 1344/5 and the Inn that they established was independent, but affiliated to the Inner Temple. It consisted of a Principal, 12 Ancients (known as 'Rules') and juniors. Illustration 135 is an engraving of the Inn's Hall, from a drawing by Thomas Shepherd, published in 1830. Illustration 136 is a print published in 1801, showing the Hall (from a slightly different angle) and the adjoining chambers. The original Hall (and most of the Inn) escaped the Great Fire of 1666 and the Judges of the Fire Court met there in 1670 to settle many of the boundary disputes arising out of the fire or disputes between landlords and tenants over responsibility for rebuilding. A new Hall was built in 1767. In 1829, it was recorded that most of the occupants of the Inn were attorneys and officers of the Marshalsea Court. No new members were admitted after 1877. The property was sold by the Rules in 1903, although many lawyers continued to occupy the buildings. The buildings were all demolished in 1935 except for the gateway that bears the arms of the Barons Clifford. John Selden (see illustration 157) and Chief Justice Edward Coke (1552-1634) were members of this Inn.

137 *(right)*
The garden front of Furnival's Inn

Furnival's Inn was on the north side of Holborn. It can be seen on Rocque's map, to the east of Gray's Inn Lane. Lord Furnival leased his town house to law students in 1383 and the property, known as Furnival's Inn after its owner, became an Inn of Chancery in about 1408. By 1422, it was affiliated to Lincoln's Inn (which purchased the freehold of the property in 1547). This print, by Samuel Ireland, was published in 1800. By 1817, Furnival's Inn had only six Ancients and 16 Juniors. It had not admitted any new members for 20 years and Lincoln's Inn refused to grant it a new lease. The old buildings of the Inn were demolished in 1820 and a new building, also known as Furnival's Inn, was built in its place. This was demolished in 1897 and replaced by the Prudential Assurance Company's building. This illustration shows the garden front of the Hall of the Inn, built in 1588. The other side of the Hall looked into the courtyard (illustration 138).

138 *(below)*
The courtyard of Furnival's Inn
This engraving of 1820 by Robert Wilkinson shows the interior courtyard of Furnival's Inn as demolition commenced, shortly after the dissolution of the Society. This view looks towards the west. The other side of the buildings, on the left, fronted on Holborn. The courtyard side of the Hall, with its cupola and bay window, is at centre right.

IX Some other scenes from Chancery Lane and Fleet Street

Chancery Lane was originally known as New Street, but became known as Chancellor's Lane in about 1377 when the House for Converted Jews (see caption to illustration 140) was taken over for the use of the Keeper of the Rolls of Chancery. Chancery Lane forms the eastern boundary of Lincoln's Inn. It is the home of the Law Society, the wig and robe-makers Ede & Ravenscroft (established in 1693), the Royal Commission on Historical Manuscripts (in Quality Court) and many firms of solicitors. An overflow courtroom for the Central Criminal Court is in Chichester Rents (named after the Bishops of Chichester who had a mansion here), on the west side of Chancery Lane.

139
The Law Society's Hall on Chancery Lane
This photograph was taken in about 1900. Chancery Lane was very much quieter in those days. A 'Society of Gentlemen Practisers in the Courts of Law and Equity' was founded in 1739 to uphold the professional standards of attorneys and solicitors. The Society met in taverns or, for a few years, in Clifford's Inn and Furnival's Inn. However, it remained a small group of London practitioners. Its membership never exceeded 200, despite there being about 7,000 attorneys and solicitors. In 1825, one of its members founded a new body for the profession – 'The Society of Attorneys, Solicitors, Proctors and others not being Barristers practising in the Courts of Law and Equity in the United Kingdom'. Fortunately, this was changed to 'The Law Society' in 1903. A hall was built, including offices, a library and members' rooms at 113 Chancery Lane in 1828. Charters were granted to the Society in 1831 and (with a coat of arms) in 1845. The hall was enlarged as adjoining properties were acquired. The Law Society remains responsible for many aspects of solicitors' education and discipline.

140
The Public Record Office on Chancery Lane
The Public Record Office (PRO) was founded by Act of Parliament in 1838 (building commenced only in 1851) to store the national archives which were then held in many different offices around London. The first part of the building was built adjacent to the Rolls Chapel. This chapel was on the site of the Chapel of the House of Converts, founded in 1232 for Jews who had converted to Christianity. After the expulsion of the Jews by Edward I, the Chapel was usually occupied by the Clerk of Chancery, who kept the records of Chancery (then a government department). He later became known as the Keeper of the Rolls of Chancery. By the reign of Henry VIII, this office was held by a lawyer and the chapel (attached to the Keeper's house) became known as the Rolls Chapel. It was not only a place of worship for the Keeper and the Masters, clerks and registrars of the Court of Chancery, but also a repository of records. The documents from the Rolls Chapel were transferred into the PRO in 1856 (records from other repositories such as the Tower of London followed). Much of the chapel was pulled down in 1895 and the remainder was incorporated into an extension to the PRO. The records at Chancery Lane were transferred to the PRO's building at Kew in 1996. The Chancery Lane building is being redeveloped for occupation by King's College.

141
El Vino at 47 Fleet Street
El Vino is perhaps the most famous of the wine bars frequented by lawyers; it is said to be the model upon which John Mortimer based Rumpole's favourite bar *Pommeroys.* Alfred Louis Bower (1856-1948) founded a wine importation business, trading under his own name, in 1879 and a wine bar soon afterwards. The name of the business was changed to El Vino in 1923. The company is still run by his family and there are now four branches in the area around Fleet Street. This drawing shows the most famous; 47 Fleet Street, opened in 1913. It is a favourite haunt for journalists, lawyers and businessmen. I was there just a few months ago, with other solicitors and Counsel, celebrating the guilty plea of an international fraudster whom we had prosecuted.

142
Sir Alfred Bower, Lord Mayor of London and the founder of El Vino
Alfred Bower's wine business originally traded under his own name. Bower was knighted in 1913 and elected Lord Mayor in 1924. It was shortly before his election (and because of the likelihood of his success) that the name of the business was changed from his own name to El Vino). Sir Alfred became Master of the Worshipful Company of Vintners in 1926.

143
The interior of *Ye Olde Cheshire Cheese,* Fleet Street
Another famous watering hole is the *Cheshire Cheese,* built soon after the Great Fire. This oak-beamed public house is on the north side of Fleet Street, with Wine Office Court on its west side. Wine Office Court took its name from the Excise Office previously located there. This postcard shows the Chop Room. To the right of the fire, above the table, can be seen the portrait of Dr. Samuel Johnson, who lived close by and is said to have dined and drunk here.

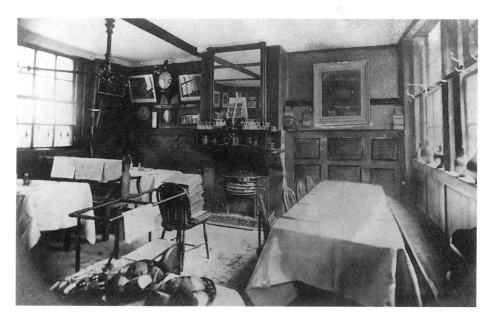

X THE LAWYERS

Lawyers have never been popular. A lawyer's epitaph in St Pancras churchyard is said to have read:

> 'Here lies ____ believe it if you can
> Who though a lawyer was an honest man,
> To him the gates of heaven shall open wide
> And quickly close against all the tribe beside.'

One of Shakespeare's characters suggested, 'Let's kill all the lawyers!'. A little harsh perhaps, and things are no doubt different today, but we remain one of the less popular professions in the view of the public. In an effort to convince the world that we are a group of kind, loving and deeply misunderstood professionals, I present a few faces of lawyers. I have included men from most parts of the legal profession; judges (of civil, criminal and ecclesiastical courts), barristers, a serjeant-at-law, Masters of the Court, a Magistrate and several solicitors. Some of these men are famous – some are now forgotten. Some of them were brilliant lawyers – some were better known for their other achievements, particularly in politics. Five of these lawyers were involved (four as barristers, one as a judge) in the case of the Tichborne claimant, one of the most famous cases of the 19th century. The matter commenced as a civil claim for ejectment by a claimant to a Baronetcy, followed by the prosecution of the claimant for perjury. Arthur Orton was the son of a Wapping butcher who claimed to be Roger Tichborne (who had been lost at sea), the son and heir of Sir James Tichborne, 10th Baronet. There was a trial, lasting 102 days, in 1871-72 of the claimant's unsuccessful action for ejectment against Sir Henry Tichborne, 12th Baronet. Orton was then tried in 1873-74 for perjury. This trial lasted 188 days and Orton was convicted and sentenced to 14 years' penal servitude (he was released after 10 years and died in poverty). Edward Kenealy (illustration 162), Leading Counsel for Orton in the perjury prosecution, was subsequently disbarred for his conduct of the case, but became a Member of Parliament.

144 *(top)*
Lord Denning, Master of the Rolls (1899-1999)
Lord Denning died in 1999. He was Master of the Rolls and dominated the Court of Appeal for 20 years. He was undoubtedly the most widely known member of the English judiciary this century (and perhaps of all time). He had a passion for justice and believed that the courts should change the law, when necessary, to meet the needs of the time, rather than simply interpret and apply it. Some of his remarks or views resulted in controversy, for example his views on homosexuality, sexual morality and hanging. However, his judgments were clear, cogent and straightforward (even if sometimes overturned by the House of Lords). Many of his judgments are considered landmarks in the development of the law (for example on the law of negligence) or resulted in his popularity with the public (for protecting the individual from misuse of power or arbitrary decisions by bureaucratic government bodies). Alfred Thompson Denning (known as Tom by his friends) was educated at Andover Grammar School and Magdalen College, Oxford. He served with the Royal Engineers in France (1917-19). He entered Lincoln's Inn and was called to the Bar in 1923, taking Silk in 1938. He was knighted and appointed as a Judge of the High Court of Justice in 1944. Denning was assigned to the Probate, Divorce and Admiralty Division then, in 1945, to the King's Bench Division. He was a Lord Justice of Appeal (1948-57), a Lord of Appeal in Ordinary (1957-62) and Master of the Rolls (1962-82). He was the author or editor of many books and he held many other posts. For example, he was Chancellor of the Diocese of London (1942-44) and of Southwark (1937-44), Chairman of the Royal Commission on Historical Manuscripts and a Bencher, then Treasurer of Lincoln's Inn. Denning also chaired the enquiry into the circumstances of the resignation of John Profumo, the Secretary of State for War, in 1963. Denning was criticised, late in his career, or after his retirement, for certain remarks that he made (for example about Britain's ethnic minorities). However, the great respect generally accorded to him is reflected in the Honorary Doctorates he received from many universities, including Ottawa, Glasgow, London, Cambridge, Dallas and Columbia. This portrait of 1974, by Edward Halliday, hangs outside the Library in Lincoln's Inn.

145 *(below left)*
Lord Halsbury, Lord Chancellor (1823-1921)
Lord Halsbury is now best remembered because his name is commemorated by the indispensable *Halsbury's Laws of England*. He presided over the production of this complete digest of English law, which was first published 1905-16 by Butterworths and is regularly updated. Hardinge Stanley Giffard was a student of Merton College, Oxford and Inner Temple. He was called to the Bar in 1850 and joined the South Wales Circuit, then practised at Middlesex Sessions House at Clerkenwell and at the Central Criminal Court in Old Bailey. He took Silk in 1865 and was one of the barristers who acted for Arthur Orton, the Tichborne claimant. Giffard was appointed Solicitor-General and knighted in 1875. He was elected as Conservative MP for Launceston in 1877 and appointed Treasurer of Inner Temple in 1881. He sat as an MP until 1885, when he was created Baron Halsbury and appointed Lord Chancellor (in which post he served 1885-86, 1886-92 and 1895-1905). He was created Viscount Tiverton and Earl of Halsbury in 1898. He was largely responsible for the Criminal Evidence Act (1898). Halsbury was also High Steward of Oxford University, Master of the Worshipful Company of Saddlers and Senior Grand Warden of English Freemasons. He was a member of the Athenaeum, Carlton and St Stephen's Clubs.

146 *(below right)*

**Lord Alverstone, Lord Chief Justice
(1842-1915)**

Richard Everard Webster, son of
Thomas Webster QC of Lincoln's
Inn, was educated at Charterhouse
and Trinity College, Cambridge. He
entered Lincoln's Inn in 1865 and
was called to the Bar in 1868. He
took Silk in 1878. He was
Conservative MP for Launceston,
then the Isle of Wight (1885-1900).
He was knighted in 1885 and was
Attorney-General 1885-86, 1886-92
and 1895-1900. He was created a
Baronet and appointed Master of
the Rolls in 1900. A few months
later, he was appointed as Lord
Chief Justice (which office he held
until 1913) and created Baron
Alverstone. He was created a
Viscount in 1913. He was President
of the M.C.C. in 1903 and of Surrey
County Cricket Club (1895-1915).
He was a member of the Carlton,
United University, Athenaeum,
Savage's and St Stephen's Clubs.

147 *(left)*
Sir Alexander Cockburn, Lord Chief Justice (1802-80)
Alexander James Edmund Cockburn studied on the continent and at Trinity Hall, Cambridge. He entered Middle Temple and was called to the Bar in 1833. He took Silk in 1841 and became MP for Southampton in 1847. He was knighted and appointed Attorney General in 1851. He became Chief Justice of the Court of Common Pleas in 1856 and succeeded his father as Baronet in 1858. He was appointed Lord Chief Justice in 1859 and presided over the Tichborne perjury trial in 1873.

148 *(below left)*
Lord Penzance (1816-99)
James Plaisted Wilde was educated at Winchester College, Trinity College, Cambridge and Inner Temple. He took Silk in 1855 and was appointed Counsel to the Duchy of Lancaster in 1859. In 1860, he was appointed Baron of the Exchequer (a judge of the Court of Exchequer) and knighted. He transferred to the Court of Probate in 1863 and was raised to the peerage, as Baron Penzance, in 1869. He retired from his judicial duties in the secular courts, due to ill health, in 1872. However, he became Dean of the Court of Arches of the Archbishop of Canterbury and also Official Principal (a judge) of the Chancery Court of York (one of the courts of the Archbishop of York) in 1875. He retired in 1899.

149 *(below right)*
Lord Selborne, Lord Chancellor (1812-95)
Roundell Palmer was educated at Rugby, Winchester and Trinity College, Oxford. He was called to the Bar (Lincoln's Inn) in 1837 and took Silk in 1849. He was elected as Conservative MP for Plymouth in 1847 but transferred to the Liberal Party. He was MP for Richmond, Yorkshire (1861-72), knighted and created Solicitor-General in 1861 and served as Attorney-General from 1863 to 1866. He was created Baron Selborne and Lord Chancellor in 1872 and was responsible for the Judicature Act 1873, which provided for the fusion of Common Law and Equity and for the reorganisation of the superior courts that took place in 1875. He was again Lord Chancellor from 1880 to 1885 and created Viscount Woolmer and Earl of Selborne. He was said to be a 'devout Churchman, a subtle and convincing lawyer and a capable politician'.

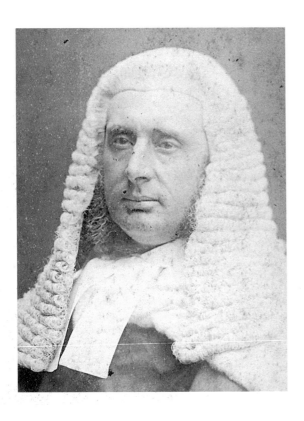

150 *(right)*

The Earl of Birkenhead, Lord Chancellor (1872-1930)

Frederick Edwin Smith studied at Wadham College, Oxford and was called to the Bar (Gray's Inn) in 1899. He began his practice in Liverpool and was a Conservative MP for Walton (1906-18). He was closely involved in the resistance to the Liberal Government's Parliament Bill and, initially, to Home Rule for Ireland. He took Silk in 1908 and was a Bencher of Gray's Inn. He was Solicitor-General in 1915 and Attorney-General from 1915 to 1919 (and engaged in the prosecution of Sir Roger Casement). Smith was Lord Chancellor (1919-22) and Secretary of State for India (1924-28). He was created Baronet in 1918, a Baron in 1919, Viscount in 1921 and 1st Earl of Birkenhead in 1922. He was a member of the Royal Automobile, Carlton and University Clubs.

151 *(below left)*

Sir Francis Jeune, Baron St Helier (1843-1905)

Francis Henry Jeune, eldest son of the Bishop of Peterborough, was educated at Harrow and at Balliol College, Oxford. He was called to the Bar (Inner Temple) in 1868. He was Counsel for the Tichborne claimant in his action for ejectment and had a large ecclesiastical practice, which resulted in him being appointed as Chancellor of the dioceses of Gloucester and Bristol. He took Silk in 1888. He was appointed a Judge of the Probate, Divorce and Admiralty Division of the High Court (and knighted) in 1891 and President of the Probate Division in 1892. He was Judge Advocate-General from 1892 to 1904. He resigned from the Bench because of ill health and was created Baron St Helier.

152 *(below right)*

The Recorder of London, Sir Ernest Wild, K.C. (1869-1934)

The Recorder is the senior law officer of the City of London – his office dates from the 13th century. He may sit as a judge in the Mayor's Court and he is the senior judge at the Central Criminal Court. Sir Edward Coke was a Recorder and the notorious Judge Jeffreys was Recorder in 1678. Ernest Edward Wild was educated at Norwich School and Jesus College, Cambridge. He was called to the Bar (Middle Temple) in 1893 and sat as a judge of the Norwich Guildhall Court of Record (1897-1922). He was MP for West Ham (1918-22) and appointed Recorder of London and High Steward of Southwark in 1922. He was also a senior Freemason.

153 *(right)*
Sir Thomas More, Lord Chancellor (1478-1535)

Thomas More was educated at Canterbury Hall, Oxford. He entered New Inn in 1494 and Lincoln's Inn in 1496 and was called to the Bar and appointed a Reader at Furnival's Inn in 1497. More became an MP in 1504 and a Bencher of Lincoln's Inn in 1509. He was appointed Under-Sheriff of London in 1510. He published *Utopia* in 1516. Henry VIII appointed More as Master of Requests and a Privy Councillor in 1518. He was knighted in 1521 and became Speaker of the House of Commons. He was appointed Lord Chancellor in 1529 and had a reputation for speedily disposing of Chancery cases. He was criticised by Protestants for his severe treatment of persons accused of heresy and resigned in 1532. More refused to take any oath recognising Henry VIII as the supreme head of the church, since that impugned the authority of the Pope. He was committed to the Tower of London and found guilty of treason at his trial in Westminster Hall in 1535. He was beheaded and his head placed on London Bridge. More was canonised in 1935.

154 *(below left)*
Lord Justice Brett (1815-99)

William Balliol Brett was educated at Westminster School and Caius College, Cambridge. He was called to the Bar (Lincoln's Inn) in 1846 and took Silk in 1861. He became MP for Helston in 1866. Brett was admitted as a Serjeant-at-Law and was Solicitor-General from February 1868 until his elevation to the Bench in August of that year. He was a Justice of the Court of Common Pleas (1868-76), a Lord Justice of Appeal (1876-83) and appointed Master of the Rolls in 1883. He died in 1899, the year in which Lord Denning was born. Brett was created Baron Esher in 1885 and Viscount Esher in 1897. He was a member of the Carlton and Athenaeum Clubs.

155 *(below right)*
Sir Joseph Chitty (1828-99)

Joseph William Chitty was educated at Eton and Balliol College, Oxford. He was called to the Bar at Lincoln's Inn in 1856 and took Silk in 1874. He was also a Major in the Inns of Court Volunteers. In 1880, he became Liberal MP for Oxford. He was knighted and appointed a Judge of the High Court (Chancery Division) in 1881 and a Lord Justice of Appeal in 1897.

156   *(above left)*

Sir Julius Caesar, Master of the Rolls (1557-1636)

Julius Caesar Aldemare was born in Tottenham in 1557, a son of Queen Mary's Italian physician, Caesar Aldemare. He preferred to use the name Caesar as his surname from an early age. He was educated at Magdalen College, Oxford and admitted as a member of Middle Temple. He obtained Doctorates of Law at both Oxford and Paris and was appointed a Judge of the Court of Admiralty in 1584. He was admitted as one of the Masters in Chancery in 1588 and became well known for assisting the poor. He was also admitted as a Master of the

Court of Requests and elected Treasurer of the Inner Temple in 1593. Caesar was knighted by James I in 1603 and elected as MP for Westminster in 1604, for Middlesex in 1614 and Malden in 1621. He became Chancellor of the Exchequer in 1606. He was also Master of the Rolls from 1614 until his death in 1636. He was buried in St Helen's Bishopgate. Caesar was said to have 'no great reputation' as a judge, but this did not prevent his promotion in the law. One of his sons, Charles, was also created Master of the Rolls (in 1639) and another son, Robert, was one of the Six Clerks in Chancery.

157   *(above right)*

John Selden (1584-1654)

Selden was educated at The Prebendal School, Chichester and Hart Hall, Oxford. He entered Clifford's Inn in 1602 and Inner Temple in 1604 and was then called to the Bar. He wrote many learned texts on aspects of the law; his work, *History of Tythes* in 1617 offended certain of the clergy and was suppressed. He was a Member of Parliament from 1623. He was Counsel to Sir Edmund Hampden, who had been committed to prison for refusing to lend money to Charles I. Selden was imprisoned in the Gatehouse (at Westminster) in 1630 for a short time for certain actions in the House of Commons. He sat on a Commons Committee in 1642 to examine the violation of the privileges of Parliament by Charles I. A monument to him at Temple Church was destroyed, but the Selden Society, which publishes historical legal material, continues to commemorate his name.

158
Mr. Granville Smith, Master of the Supreme Court (1859-1925)
Granville Smith was born in Dartmouth, the son of William Smith, a Solicitor and Notary. He was educated at Blundell's School, Tiverton and qualified as a Solicitor. He worked as a Master in the Taxing Office of the Supreme Court and was a member of the Royal Automobile Club and of the Worshipful Company of Woolmen.

159
Mr. John Tanner, Taxing Master of the High Court in Bankruptcy (1854-1928)
John Arthur Charles Tanner was educated at Marlborough and at St John's College, Oxford. He was Assistant Solicitor to the Official Receiver in Bankruptcy and then a Taxing Master of the High Court in Bankruptcy.

160
Henry Rooth, J.P. (1861-1928)
Henry Goodwin Rooth was educated at Harrow and Trinity College, Cambridge. He entered Inner Temple and was called to the Bar in 1887. He practised at London Sessions and on the South Eastern Circuit, often for the Director of Public Prosecutions. He was Metropolitan Police Court Magistrate and Justice of the Peace for the six Home Counties from 1917. He was a member of the Garrick, Arts and Royal Automobile Clubs.

161
William Ballantine, Serjeant-at-Law (1812-87)
William Ballantine was educated at St Paul's School and called to the Bar (Inner Temple) in 1834. He became a Serjeant-at-Law in 1856, being sworn on 9 June in the Lord Chancellor's room at the House of Lords. He conducted the prosecution in 1864 of Franz Muller (see caption to illustration 56). Ballantine was also Leading Counsel for Arthur Orton, the Tichborne claimant, at the trial of his action for ejectment against Sir Henry Tichborne.

162
Edward Kenealy QC (1819-80)
Edward Vaughan Hyde Kenealy studied at Trinity College, Dublin and was called to the Irish Bar in 1840. He was called to the English Bar (Gray's Inn) in 1847 and took Silk in 1868. He was Leading Counsel for Arthur Orton, the Tichborne claimant, at his trial in 1873-74 for perjury. Kenealy was disbarred for his conduct of the case. He was Member of Parliament for Stoke on Trent (1875-80).

163
Herbert Henry Asquith, Earl of Oxford and Asquith (1852-1928)
Herbert Henry Asquith was born in Morley, Yorkshire and educated at the City of London School and Balliol College, Oxford. He entered Lincoln's Inn and was called to the Bar in 1876, taking Silk in 1890. He was Liberal MP for East Fife (1886-1918) and Home Secretary (1892-95). He returned to his practice at the Bar during the Liberals' term of opposition (1895-1905). He was Chancellor of the Exchequer (1905-08) and Prime Minister (1908-16). He was created Earl of Oxford and Asquith in 1925 and was a member of Brook's, the Athenaeum and the Reform Club.

164
Viscount Simon, Lord Chancellor (1873-1954)
John Allsebrook Simon was educated at Bath Grammar School, Fettes College, Edinburgh and Wadham College, Oxford. He was called to the Bar (Inner Temple) in 1899, taking Silk in 1908. He was a Member of Parliament (1906-18 and 1922-40) and was knighted and became Solicitor-General in 1910 in the Liberal government. He was appointed Attorney-General in 1913 and Home Secretary in 1915. He resigned in opposition to the introduction of conscription. He formed the Liberal National Party in 1931 and served as Foreign Secretary (1931-35), Home Secretary (1935-37) and Chancellor of the Exchequer (1937-40). He was created Viscount Simon in 1940 and served as Lord Chancellor (1940-45) He was a member of the Reform, Garrick, National Liberal and Royal Automobile Clubs.

165

Sir William Bull, solicitor and MP (1863-1931)
William Bull was senior partner in the firm of Bull & Bull, solicitors of Stone Buildings, Lincoln's Inn and also a director of Siemens Bros. and Co. Ltd. He was admitted as a solicitor in 1889. He was a member of London County Council from 1892 to 1901 and Conservative MP for South Hammersmith (1900 and 1918-29). He was knighted in 1905 and created a Baronet in 1922. He was also a member of the Council of the Law Society, President of the Royal Albert Hall and a member of the Carlton and Constitutional Clubs.

166

Mr. Walter Bartlett, solicitor
Walter Bartlett was senior partner of the firm of Palmer, Bull, Bartlett & Co., solicitors of Bedford Row. After serving his articles in Chichester, he came to London in 1877 and was admitted as a solicitor in 1878. He served as Under-Sheriff for Sussex and as Deputy Sheriff of Kent. He described his chief recreations as golf and croquet.

167

Sir George Lewis, solicitor (1868-1927)
George James Graham Lewis was educated at Harrow and Balliol College, Oxford and admitted as a solicitor in 1894. He became senior partner of the firm of Lewis & Lewis of Ely Place, Holborn (he was the third generation of his family to head this firm). He also succeeded as Baronet on the death of his father in 1911. He was a member of the Bath and Royal Automobile Clubs.

168

Mr. Arthur Horner, solicitor
Arthur Horner was the son of a Bristol solicitor, educated both privately and at Bristol Cathedral School. He was admitted as a solicitor and worked for the firm of Lewis & Lewis of Holborn. He listed his recreations as literature, golf and fishing, but also attributed his good health to the fact that he had never played an athletic game in his life. This ensured his inclusion in this sample of lawyers.

169
Sir George Allen, solicitor (1888-1956)
Albert George Allen was educated at
North Malvern School and served in
France from 1914 to 1919 as a
Captain in the South Staffordshire
regiment, then as Brigade Major in
the 51st Infantry Brigade. He was
awarded the Distinguished Service
Order and Military Cross and was
mentioned in despatches twice. He
founded Allen & Overy in 1930 with
Thomas Overy in a small office at 3
Finch Lane in the City of London.
Allen & Overy is not one of the
oldest firms of solicitors in the City
of London, but it does illustrate
some of the enormous changes that
have occurred in the legal
profession, particularly in the 17
years in which I was a solicitor at the
firm. Allen & Overy is one of the
London firms that have developed
into large multinational
organisations within the course of
only a few years. From its small
beginnings, it has grown into one of
the largest firms in the world, with
220 partners, 735 assistant solicitors
(and a total staff of 2,470). In
addition to the London office, the
firm has 19 offices throughout the
world (including Hong Kong, New
York, Moscow, Paris, Beijing, Dubai,
Tokyo and even Tirana). Staff in
each office are connected to
everyone else by e-mail, fast
telephone systems and video-
conferencing facilities. A few
historical points are worth noting.
Christopher Walford, a partner in
the firm from 1970 to 1996, was
Master of the City of London
Solicitors' Company (founded in
1908) and elected Lord Mayor of
the City of London in 1994. Lawyers
of the firm have always acted in a
large number of important
corporate, financial, property,
private or litigious matters. However,
in 1936, George Allen acted in
perhaps the most important
constitutional matter of the century,
advising Edward VIII during the
abdication crisis. Allen continued to
act for him, as Duke of Windsor,
after the abdication. George Allen
was created KCVO in 1952 and
retired in 1953. An interesting
history of Allen & Overy has recently
been published and is noted in the
bibliography.

170 *(above)*
Sir Thomas Overy, solicitor (1893-1973)
Thomas Stuart Overy was educated
at Kent College, Canterbury. He
served in the Royal Fusiliers and the
Buffs in France from 1914 to 1918,
being promoted to Captain. He was
admitted as a solicitor in 1921. He
was George Allen's partner at the
founding of Allen & Overy in 1930.
He was joint senior partner with
Allen, then sole Senior Partner from
1953. He was knighted in 1954 and
retired in 1960.

171 *(above right)*
**George Allen leaving 10 Downing
Street during the abdication crisis of
1936**

172 *(below)*
**King Edward VIII broadcasting to
the Empire**
This postcard records his first
broadcast as King. A few months
later, in December 1936, a similar
picture was taken of Edward VIII, but
this time he was giving his abdication
speech.

173 *(top left)*
Members of the judiciary leaving Westminster Abbey
On the re-opening of the Royal Courts of Justice on the first day of the Michaelmas Term, after the Long Vacation, the Lord Chancellor presides over a breakfast at the House of Lords and there is then a service at Westminster Abbey. The service is attended by the Lords Justices, High Court Judges, County Court Judges, Queen's Counsel and members of the Junior Bar. For many years, the service was followed by a procession to the Courts for their formal opening.

174 *(below left)*
Ward Beadles of the City of London
A beadle was a parish or ward officer. He was responsible for supervision of the Watch and taverns, he summoned parishioners to attend meetings of the Vestry, he kept children in order (with a cane if necessary), he whipped vagrants and he generally assisted with the administration of the poor law. This photograph shows the beadles of ten of the 36 wards of the City of London in about 1925.

175 *(right)*
Panyer man in the Temple
For centuries, the Panyer man summoned members of the Middle Temple to dinner in the Hall with a silver-mounted ox-horn. His title derived from an ancient duty of fetching bread.

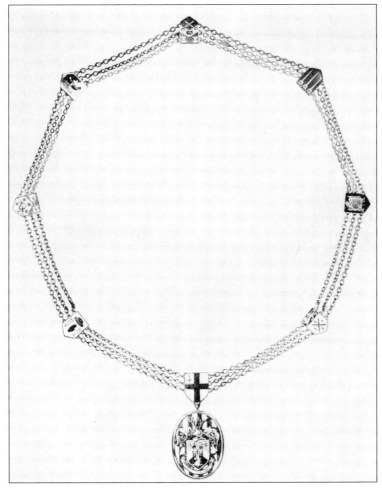

176
Regalia of a sheriff of the City of London
The office of Sheriff dates from the 11th century. The Sheriffs attend on the Lord Mayor for many of his official functions and attend sessions of the Central Criminal Court. They also used to control and supervise the City prisons known as Compters (see illustrations 192-94) and appoint the hangmen at Tyburn and Newgate. This is the chain and badge of office of George McKay, elected as Sheriff in 1921. The chain was made of 18-carat gold and was adorned with shields bearing McKay's coat of arms and the arms of the City of London and of some of the London Livery companies.

XI THE LAWYERS' CHURCHES

Many of the churches of London are associated with the law and lawyers. Temple Church, St Mary-le-Strand and the chapels of Lincoln's Inn and Gray's Inn have already been noted.

177

St Clement Danes and the Royal Courts of Justice

St Clement Danes probably takes its name from an old church on the site, in which some Danes were buried in the 9th or 10th centuries (or which was possibly built by Danes who were permitted to reside in the area). The church had pews that were reserved for members of Clement's Inn. It escaped damage in

209365 J.V.   St. Cleme

the Great Fire but was rebuilt in 1681 to a design by Wren. It now stands on an island in the middle of the Strand at the western end of the Royal Courts of Justice. It has only been an island since 1810, when some houses on the north side were demolished. This postcard view looks to the east, with the courts on the left and the dome of St Paul's Cathedral in the distance on the right. The wedding-cake steeple of St Bride's can also be seen, just to the left of St Paul's. St Clement Danes was badly damaged during the Blitz. The steeple survived and the remainder of the church was restored. It is now the Central Church for the RAF and holds a roll of honour for British and Commonwealth airmen (and many Americans) who died in action in WW2.

Danes Church and Fleet Street, London (120)

178

St Andrew's Holborn

St Andrew's Holborn was built in the 12th century, possibly on the site of an earlier church dedicated to St Andrew. It escaped the Great Fire, but was dilapidated and so rebuilt by Wren in 1686. St Andrew's was badly damaged during the Blitz, but rebuilt. Many lawyers attended this church and were married or buried here. Sir Edward Coke, Chief Justice to James I and Charles I married here in 1598. The members of Barnard's Inn had their own pews in the church. There were so many burials that a further burial ground for the church was opened in Gray's Inn Road. In March 1819, a parishioner named Mr. Gilbert wished to bury his wife in that burial yard in a coffin made of iron (because she had dreaded that her remains might be despoiled by bodysnatchers). The rector and vestry refused to do so unless Gilbert paid a special fee of £10. Gilbert applied to the Court of King's Bench for an order of mandamus to the minister and churchwardens of St Andrew's to bury the corpse without any fee. The court refused to make the order because it was an ecclesiastical matter (for the church courts to decide). Gilbert's petition to Parliament was ignored. The matter finally came before the Bishop of London's Consistory Court in 1820. That court held that the durability of iron coffins was unfair to others who might wish to be buried in the graveyard, so this justified a higher fee. However, St Andrew's had not obtained prior court approval for the fees, so the court recommended that there should be no fee on this occasion. In November 1820, Mrs Gilbert and her iron coffin (in St Andrew's 'bone-house' for 20 months) were finally buried.

179

St Sepulchre, Newgate

St Sepulchre's Church is on the north side of Holborn. It stood opposite Newgate Gaol (and now the Central Criminal Court). The church was originally named St Edmund without Newgate or St Edmund Sepulchre (dedicated to the East Anglian King and Martyr). John Rogers, a Protestant rector of this church, was imprisoned in Newgate and burned at Smithfield in 1554, for calling Queen Mary's religion 'pestilent popery, idolatry and superstition'. Captain John Smith (whose life was saved by the Indian Princess Pocahontas) was buried here. In 1605, Robert Dowe gave the sum of £50 to the church for ringing the church bell when condemned prisoners at Newgate Gaol were to be executed. Dowe also requested the sexton to go to Newgate on the eve of executions, ring his bell outside the condemned cell and cry out:

All you that in the condemned hold do lie,
Prepare you, for tomorrow you shall die,
Watch all, and pray, the hour is drawing
   near
That you before the Almighty must appear;
Examine well yourselves, in time repent,
That you may not to eternal flames be sent,
And when St Sepulchre's bell tomorrow
   tolls,
The Lord above have mercy on your souls.

Well, that must have cheered them up! As the execution procession left Newgate for Tyburn, the church bell tolled and a nosegay was presented to each prisoner. St Sepulchre was badly damaged in the Great Fire, but rebuilt. It escaped serious damage in WW2 and was dedicated, in 1949, to all men who have served in the Royal Fusiliers (City of London Regiment).

XII THE PRISONS OF LONDON

London had more prisons than any other English city, partly because of its greater population, but also because of the location in London of the central courts. The Tower of London was noted at the start of this book and Brixton Prison and the Hulks, moored in the Thames, are included in the following section. Many other prisons are included in this section, such as Newgate Gaol, Bridewell, Ludgate, the Fleet, Millbank Penitentiary and the Houses of Correction and Detention in Clerkenwell. Some of the more modern prisons are also featured, such as Wandsworth and Holloway. Many prisons were located in Southwark. The Marshalsea, King's Bench, Horsemonger Lane Gaol and others are featured below. Some lesser-known prisons are also featured, such as the City Compters. The name Compter derives from 'counter', the counting or keeping of official records. The Compters were prisons under the control of the two Sheriffs of the City of London. They were principally intended for debtors, and also for drunks, vagrants and, on occasion, other prisoners.

Readers may be surprised at the large number of prisons intended for debtors (or that debtors were imprisoned at all). The Crown commenced imprisoning those who owed it money in the 12th century; partly as punishment and partly to encourage debtors to pay in the future. The law gradually extended the power of imprisonment to civil debts. A creditor could obtain a warrant for imprisonment upon swearing that the debt was due. The gaols began to fill up very quickly. Those men who were truly insolvent might spend years in prison, unable to afford to clear the debt. The process of bankruptcy – clearing the slate for a percentage of all the debts due – was only available to traders. Legislation in the 19th century allowed all men to go into bankruptcy and abolished imprisonment for debt (except where it was proved that a man had the means, but refused, to pay a valid debt).

I have had to omit certain prisons for lack of space. The 'Tun', a building in Cornhill, was used as a prison from 1282 to 1401 for those who broke the curfew then in force in the City. Ely Place, on Holborn, was a grand town house of the Bishops of Ely. It had a chapel and some rooms were used as a prison. Much of the building was used as a prison during the Civil War. It was demolished in 1772.

The Clink Prison (which resulted in the slang 'in the clink') originated in cells within the palace of the Bishop of Winchester in Southwark, just to the south of Bankside. It was used for clergymen and local offenders, including those who committed offences or breached the peace around the brothels on Bankside, which were licensed and supervised by the Bishop until 1504. The palace was rebuilt in the 14th century, and a new prison was built next to the palace. The dungeons had manacles, chains and fetters to hold prisoners securely (and in discomfort). The 'clinking and clanking' of these may have given the prison its name. The gaolers extorted money from prisoners and tortured them. Prostitution carried on inside the Clink, with a share of the proceeds being paid to the Keeper of the prison. A pillory and ducking-stool were also located outside the prison for the punishment of offenders. In the 16th century, the Clink remained the Bishop of Winchester's prison and held many Catholics and Protestants, such as William Hooper, Bishop of London, before his execution in 1555. It continued to be used for local offenders. Debtors were also incarcerated there. The 'Common' side of the prison had bare beds, which were full of vermin. The only food was that which arrived as Alms. Many prisoners were naked and suffered from disease. The 'Hole' was a dark, rat-infested dungeon where many prisoners were left to die. The Clink became so decayed that it was little used by 1720. From 1745, a dwelling-house on Bankside was used in its stead. This was burned down in the Gordon Riots of 1780 and never rebuilt. The Clink Exhibition is on the site of the prison and open to the public.

The Gatehouse Prison was built in about 1370 over two gates, at right angles to each other, at Westminster Abbey. One gate looked to the north and included the Bishop of London's prison for convicted clerics. The other gate looked to the west and included a gaol for lay offenders. Sir Walter Raleigh spent his last night here in 1618 before his execution in Old Palace Yard, Westminster. John Selden (see illustration 157) was a prisoner here in 1630. Samuel Pepys was held here for three weeks in 1690 'on suspicion of being affected to King James'. The Gatehouse was demolished in 1776.

Bread Street Compter was built in the early 15th century. Richard Husband, the Keeper of the Compter, was so cruel to prisoners that he was gaoled briefly in Newgate in 1550. He returned to his post and previous practices. He also offered cells as cheap overnight accomodation for thieves and prostitutes. The City authorities closed the Compter in 1555 and transferred the prisoners to a new Compter on Wood Street.

Wellclose Square (also known as Neptune Street Prison) was a small prison for the court of the Liberty of the Tower of London, a small area beyond the moat of the Tower. This old town house included the court and a tavern as well as the prison. It originally held debtors but later held prisoners awaiting trial. The Liberty of the Tower lost its criminal jurisdiction in the 19th century and the prison became a lodging-house.

Wormwood Scrubs was built in the shape of four parallel blocks by convict labour (and completed in 1890) to hold 1,000 inmates, the largest prison in Britain. It originally held both men and women but has held only men since 1902.

The London

Amongst the Works which Nature
As well for Admiration as for
A most surprizing Ostrich her
By Nature large & largest of its
His Height Prodigious but abo
He hardest Steel or Iron can

180

Newgate in the early 18th century
Newgate was one of the gates of Roman London. There was a prison over the gate from the 12th century or possibly earlier. It was a prison for both the City of London and Middlesex, in the charge of the Sheriffs of London and Middlesex, who appointed the Keeper of the prison (often selling the office to the highest bidder). Conditions were very poor; some prisoners were held in deep dungeons, and often tortured. In 1414, the Keeper of Newgate and 64 inmates died of plague. In 1449, the Keeper was imprisoned for raping a female prisoner. Newgate was burned down in the Great Fire and rebuilt in 1672.

Conditions remained miserable. There were frequent outbreaks of gaol fever, a form of typhoid. The dungeons remained in use for those who could not afford to pay for the less unpleasant cells. In the mid-18th century, a windmill was placed on top of the structure, to provide some ventilation to the cells below. The gate was demolished in 1777.

The execution at Tyburn of Prior Houghton and three monks of Charterhouse was noted above (see caption to illustration 54). Twenty monks then signed the Oath of Supremacy but 11 other monks were imprisoned in Newgate. They were chained upright in a dungeon and 10 died from filth and disease. The survivor, William Horn, was

transferred to the Tower until his execution at Tyburn three years later. Daniel Defoe was a prisoner in Newgate for a period in 1702/3.

This engraving was executed in about 1750 and was entitled 'The London rairey shows or who'll step into Ketch's Theatre'. It contains a fine view of the gate, with a menagerie on the right and a row of shops on the left. Jack Sheppard is shown imprisoned in the gatehouse and Jonathan Wild is at the door,

ey Shows or who'll step into Ketch's Theatre.

	Newgate appears & how John Sheppard lay	But here's one thing to be admir'd the most
oduce	In heavy Irons till the fatal Day	Of which the earliest Ages cannot boast
d	The crowding Populace flock in to see	Nor England ever had the same before
	This Man who did the Jail and Law defy	Two Lions young brought forth in LondonTower
t	Who twice being taken twice did make escape	The like of this in such a Northern Clime
	But now He's caught & Tyburn is his Fate	Has not been known since the first date of time

besieged by a crowd of people seeking the return of their stolen property. Jack Ketch was a well-known hangman at Tyburn from 1663 to 1686, who also bungled the beheading of the Duke of Monmouth at Tower Hill in 1685 by using a blunt axe. After three attempts, Ketch had to use a knife to remove Monmouth's head. All Tyburn hangmen were thenceforth popularly known as 'Jack Ketch'. Newgate was also the scene of two

famous escapes by Jack Sheppard (1702-24). His first escape, with a woman known as Edgeworth Bess, was by use of a rope made of blankets and sheets. He escaped a second time despite being handcuffed, manacled and chained to the floor. Sheppard was again recaptured and returned to Newgate. He was placed in the 'Condemned Hold', where he was seen by hundreds of paying sightseers, before being executed at

Tyburn in 1724. Jonathan Wild was the self-styled 'Thief-Taker-General'; he found stolen property and sent many criminals to the gallows, but he also had informants, prostitutes and pickpockets working for him and he controlled gangs of thieves and burglars, and had warehouses in which to store the loot. Finally, in 1725, Wild took his journey in the cart from Newgate to Tyburn.

181

The burning of Newgate Gaol in 1780, during the Gordon riots

Newgate was demolished in 1777. The prisoners were moved into an adjacent new building, designed by George Dance the Younger, at the top of the street named Old Bailey. This gaol was damaged by fire during the Gordon Riots of 1780 (protesting against the repeal of legislation that discriminated against Catholics) as shown in this drawing from *Old and New London*, based on a contemporary print. The gaol was rebuilt and subsequently modified, but it was overcrowded, poorly ventilated and dark. One of the early prisoners was Lord George Gordon (an M.P. and leader of the Protestant Association). He had been acquitted of high treason after the riots but was subsequently imprisoned for libelling the government. He died of gaol fever in Newgate in 1793. Conditions were poor. The Quaker, Elizabeth Fry, began visiting the female side of the prison in 1813

and was so shocked by the sight of starving, drunk women lying on the stone floor for lack of bedding, that she began her campaign for reform. Despite this, conditions remained harsh throughout the 19th century. The debtors' side of the gaol was built for 100; but 340 were there in 1873. The female felons' ward was built for 60, but 120 were there in 1873. Drink was freely sold within the gaol and many of the gaolers were found to have committed extortion and oppression, or sold 'access' to the female section. Public hangings took place outside the gaol, after they ceased at Tyburn, until 1868. In 1852, the opening of Holloway Prison resulted in Newgate only being used for the custody of prisoners awaiting trial at the Old Bailey, or those awaiting execution. Newgate was demolished in 1902 and some of the stones from it were used in the construction of the Central Criminal Court, which was built on the site.

182 *(left)*
Newgate Gaol, *c.*1898
This photograph shows the grim exterior of the gaol. It was deliberately designed to look like a fortress. It also resembles a tomb; which it in fact was for many of those who were condemned to death (see illustration 184). This photograph was taken from a rooftop, looking east, so that the dome of St Paul's Cathedral can be seen in the background.

183 *(above)*
A warder in Newgate Gaol, *c.*1898

184

Dead man's walk, Newgate Gaol
Illustrations 184 to 188 are part of a
series of postcards, called *Glimpses of
Old Newgate*, that were published at
the turn of the century. It is difficult
to imagine who would want to send
such cards (or receive them), but
public interest in executions
remained high (and remains so
today). Birdcage Walk in Newgate
Gaol was also known as Dead man's
walk. It was the last walking place of
those awaiting execution and it was a
burial ground for executed
prisoners. They were buried under
the paving slabs of this passageway,
which connected the gaol and the
adjoining Sessions House. Those
who had been sentenced to death
therefore walked over the stones,
knowing that they would soon lie
under them.

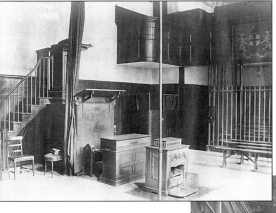

185 *(above)*
Interior of the chapel of Newgate Gaol
In the 18th and early 19th centuries, there might be up to 50 prisoners at Newgate at any one time who had been convicted of a capital crime and who awaited the death warrant. They were given only bread and water and were obliged to attend the chapel on the Sunday before their execution, where they were confronted by a black coffin and the notorious 'Death Sermon'.

186 *(above right)*
The waiting box and the execution shed at Newgate Gaol
This is another cheerful postcard, from *Glimpses of Old Newgate*, upon which some lively greeting could be written. From 1868, executions took place in the timber shed on the right of this photograph.

187 *(right)*
Inside one of the cell blocks at Newgate Gaol

188 *(below right)*
The gallows in the execution shed at Newgate Gaol
A condemned prisoner stood on the closed trapdoor with a noose around his neck. The rope was attached to the chain on the beam above and the trapdoor then dropped open and the prisoner hanged. I wonder if anyone ever sent this postcard with the message 'wish you were here'?

The quadrangle, male prison, female prison and Great Hall of Bridewell

Henry VIII built a palace at Bridewell where the Fleet River flowed into the Thames. Within a few years, the dissolution of the monasteries was causing problems. The poor and sick, who previously relied on alms from the monasteries, now had no means of support except charity. The number of beggars increased and they were said to be 'swarming in the streets'. Petty theft and other crime also increased. Bridewell Palace, by then little used, was therefore granted by Edward VI to the Corporation of the City of London for use as a 'Hospital', but for 'moral, not physical deformities'. It was to be used to deal with vagrants, petty offenders and 'disorderly women'. Poverty and sickness were seen no differently from crime and were dealt with severely. The 'Hospital' was opened on 16 December 1556, on which day a woman was whipped at Bridewell, then placed in the pillory at Cheapside, for having abandoned her baby on the streets. Bridewell became a 'House of Correction and House of Occupation', punishing wrongdoers and putting vagrants and beggars to work. In the next few years, many Roman Catholics and non-conformists were also imprisoned there. Bridewell was famous for chastising vagrants (they were whipped on arrival). In 1628 and 1638, a ducking-stool and a whipping-post were installed. Large crowds gathered twice a week for the public floggings of half-naked prisoners. The regime of Bridewell (and its name) was copied elsewhere in London, for example at Westminster and Clerkenwell and in many other places in England. Most of the buildings of Bridewell were destroyed in the Great Fire, but rebuilt. The flogging of women was abolished in 1791 and the prison was closed in 1855 (the last prisoners were transferred to Holloway Prison). Most of the buildings were demolished in 1863. Much of the site is now occupied by the Unilever Building. This engraving, from a drawing by Thomas Shepherd, published in 1822, shows the quadrangle with parts of the male and the female prisons and a part of the Great Hall.

190 *(below left)*

Bridewell

This engraving provides a bird's-eye view of Bridewell. The stocks can be seen against the wall in the nearest courtyard.

191 *(top right)*

Ludgate

This was another gate of the City of London over which there was a prison. The Romans probably built a gate on the site. In 1260, the gate was adorned with images of the mythical King Lud and his two sons. A prison was built inside the gate in the late 14th century and enlarged in 1443. It was used for petty offenders, debtors, freemen of the City of London and clergymen. As in most of the debtors' prisons, the gaolers obtained money from the prisoners by way of fees; for lodging, turning the key (on entry or discharge) or for food. The gate was rebuilt in 1586 and again after the Great Fire. It was demolished in 1760 and prisoners were then held in a workhouse on Bishopsgate Street, until that was closed in 1794. This drawing, from *Old and New London*, shows Ludgate in about 1750.

192 *(below left)*
Wood Street Compter, c.1793
Wood Street Compter was built in 1555 (to replace that in Bread Street) to hold 70 prisoners. It was rebuilt in 1670, after the Great Fire. It had three sections; the 'Masters' side' for the wealthy, the 'Knights' side' for the comfortably off and the 'Hole' for the poor. Those who had money would pay the Keeper and gaolers for better quarters, food and drink. The office of Keeper of the Compter was therefore very profitable and was bought and sold until the 18th century. Some inmates, such as attorneys and physicians, continued to trade from inside the prison so as to maintain themselves. Jonathan Wild, the 'Thief-taker General', was imprisoned here from 1710 to 1712. In 1776, the Compter was described as dark and full of filth and vermin. It was closed in 1791 and replaced by Giltspur Street Compter. This drawing, from *Old and New London*, was based on a print of 1793.

193 *(below right)*
Poultry Compter
Poultry Compter was the oldest of the City Compters, having been built in the 14th century. It was rebuilt in 1615, destroyed in the Great Fire but again rebuilt. In the late 17th century, the smell in Poultry Compter was said to be worse than a Southwark ditch and the inmates were described as 'ill-looking vermin, with long rusty beards, swaddled up in rags'. The enormous key to the Compter door can be seen in the hand of the gaoler, in the doorway, in this engraving. Poultry Compter was demolished in 1817.

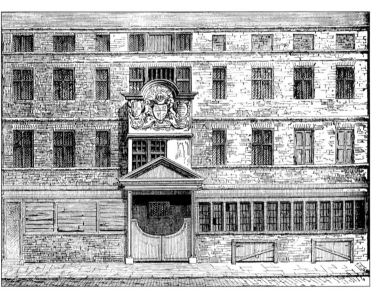

194 *(left)*
Giltspur Street Compter
Giltspur Street Compter was opened in 1791 opposite St Sepulchre's Church, Newgate (see illustration 179) for debtors, felons and 'nightcharges', to replace Wood Street Compter. The debtors were transferred to the City's debtor prison in Whitecross Street in 1815 and Giltspur Street was then used as a House of Correction for male and female beggars and vagrants. It was closed in 1854, being replaced by the City's new House of Correction at Holloway. This engraving of about 1830 is from a drawing by Thomas Shepherd.

The front of the Fleet Prison

The Fleet Prison is perhaps the best known of the London debtor prisons. It was built in the 12th century on an island formed by the Fleet River and ditches. By the 14th century, these were all full of stagnant and foul water. In the early years, the prison was also used for those in contempt of the Royal Courts and (in Tudor and Stuart times) those convicted in the Court of Star Chamber. Distinguished prisoners in the 16th and 17th centuries included the Earl of Surrey in 1543, William Herbert, Earl of Pembroke in 1601 and the poet John Donne, later Dean of St Paul's Cathedral, also in 1601. The Fleet was later used principally to hold bankrupts and debtors. Debtors begged for money from passers-by through a heavily barred window. The Fleet was also the scene of much cruelty, extortion, drunkenness and depravity. The office of Keeper, or Warden, of the Fleet was hereditary. It included the right to receive fees from prisoners for their food, lodging or for short-term release into the lawless area surrounding the prison known as 'Rules' or 'Liberties' of the Fleet. The Keeper of the Fleet made so much money out of the inmates that one Huggins purchased the office in the early 18th century for £5,000 (and then extorted enormous fees from prisoners). The poorer inmates might lose their last possessions or hand over any proceeds of begging, or money received from family and friends. Some inmates could afford the fees: the Fleet usually held some wealthy men who had run up large debts and used the Fleet to hide temporarily from their creditors. The Fleet had some pleasures for the wealthy. It had a tap room and a coffee-room and racquets was played in the courtyard. One writer called the Fleet the largest brothel in England. Huggins later sold his office to a solicitor, Thomas Bambridge, also for £5,000. A Parliamentary Commission found Bambridge guilty of extortion, arbitrarily putting prisoners in dungeons or otherwise treating them in the 'most cruel and barbarous manner'. However, there was little improvement in the conditions in the prison. In 1774, the Fleet held 243 prisoners (mostly debtors) and 475 others (mostly the debtors' wives and children). Many of the men,

women and children lived in dirty conditions with no medical attention, particularly in the cellar, named 'Bartholomew Fair', where the poorest prisoners lodged. Men and women drank heavily and mixed freely. The Fleet was burned in the Peasant's Revolt of 1381, in the Great Fire and in the Gordon Riots of 1780 but rebuilt each time. When it was closed in 1842, one of the prisoners had been there for 28 years. The Fleet was also a popular venue for clandestine marriages (that is without licence or banns) from about 1680 until 1754. Marriages were performed in the prison chapel (for fees payable to the prison chaplain and warders) and

then in marriage houses established in taverns and private houses in the Rules of the Fleet. As many as 70 clergymen worked in the Fleet marriage trade over this period. Some of these ministers may have been imprisoned for debt; others had no benefices to support them or were simply attracted to the Fleet by the easy money to be made. Some became rich from the fees that they charged. The Fleet marriage registers, recording about 350,000 weddings, are held at the Public Record Office and are gradually being transcribed and published.

196
A courtyard of the Fleet Prison

century, the hospital declined and criminals stayed there, or in its grounds, claiming sanctuary from the law. The buildings were gradually converted to other uses, including an army barracks. A military prison was built on one part of the site in 1695. It was used to hold offenders (such as men who had tried deserting). It also held men who had been pressed into the Army (until they were sent to regiments abroad), or convicts who were granted (and took) the option of military service over hanging. Daniel Defoe stated that the Savoy also included a civil prison, called 'The Dutchy', possibly named after the Duchy of Lancaster. The hospital (now much reduced in size) was dissolved in 1702. The barracks were burned down in 1776, but the prison survived about another 20 years. The site is now occupied by the *Savoy Hotel*, the Savoy Theatre and Embankment Gardens.

197 *(above)*
The Rake in the Fleet Prison
This engraving of the inside of the Fleet comes from Hogarth's series, the 'Rake's Progress'.

198 *(below left)*
The Savoy
The Savoy was a palace between the Thames and the Strand, occupied by a son of the Count of Savoy in the 13th century. It later passed to the Earls and Dukes of Lancaster (and became the headquarters of the great Duchy of Lancaster). In the early 16th century, the palace was restored and became a hospital, with a chapel. However, in the late 16th

199 *(below)*
The interior of White Lyon Prison, Southwark
The White Lyon was a small gaol for the county of Surrey, situated on Borough High Street, near the Marshalsea and King's Bench Prisons. It was probably an inn that was converted into a gaol in the 16th century and it does not appear to have been used after about 1700. This watercolour of 1887, long after the demise of the gaol, was by John Crowther.

200
Whitecross Street Prison

Concerns about the imprisonment of debtors in Newgate, where they mixed with felons, and the poor conditions at Poultry Compter resulted in the Corporation of London erecting a prison in Whitecross Street in 1813-15 to accommodate 490 debtors. Whitecross Street runs south from Old Street to Chiswell Street. The prison was demolished in 1870 after imprisonment for debt was abolished. The Barbican Arts Centre now covers the site. This watercolour of about 1840 by Frederick Napoleon Shepherd (1819-78) shows the front of the prison.

201
King's Bench Prison, Southwark

There were two King's Bench Prisons. The first was built in the 14th century to the east of Borough High Street, to hold prisoners on behalf of the Court of King's Bench. John Rushworth, Clerk of the House of Commons, died there as a prisoner in 1690. Many of the inmates were debtors. The conditions in the prison depended on the finances of the prisoner (and his family and friends). An inquiry of 1754 revealed many irregularities in the prison, including filth, overcrowding, extortion and cruelty by the gaolers, and promiscuity and drunkenness amongst the prisoners. The wealthy lived in relative comfort. The second King's Bench Prison, with 224 rooms and a courtyard, was built in St George's Fields to the south west, on the corner of the present Borough Road and Borough High Street. John Wilkes was imprisoned here from 1768 to 1770 for libel, and Lord Cochrane (found guilty of Stock Exchange frauds) in 1815. Theodore, King of Corsica settled in London in 1749 after he was driven from his throne. He was arrested for debt in 1752 and held in the King's Bench Prison, dying in 1756, just after his release. Poor prisoners survived by holding out a begging-box at the gate. Rich prisoners lived comfortably, taking advantage of the prison's taproom, wine room and market (including a chandler's shop, a butcher's shop and a surgery). There were also up to 30 gin shops. A historian described the prison, in 1828, as 'the most desirable place of incarceration in England'. For a small fee, a prisoner could obtain leave of absence for a few days. For a large payment, some prisoners were allowed to live in the 'Liberties' or 'Rules', an area surrounding the prison that included many taverns. After the accession of Queen Victoria, the King's Bench was merged with the Marshalsea and Fleet prisons and renamed the Queen's Bench Prison. Following the abolition of imprisonment for debt, Queen's Bench was used as a military prison, then demolished in 1880. This engraving of about 1820, from a drawing by Thomas Shepherd, shows the entrance to the second King's Bench Prison.

The Marshalsea Prison

The Marshalsea Prison in Southwark was probably built in the 14th century. Its name derives from the court once held by the Steward and Marshal of the Royal Household. This court moved with the King during his travels round the realm and had jurisdiction for 12 miles around his lodging (members of the King's Household were therefore subject to the King's court rather than a local one). The prison was originally used to serve this court. Gratwick, one of the Protestant martyrs, was held here in 1557, then burned in St George's Fields after

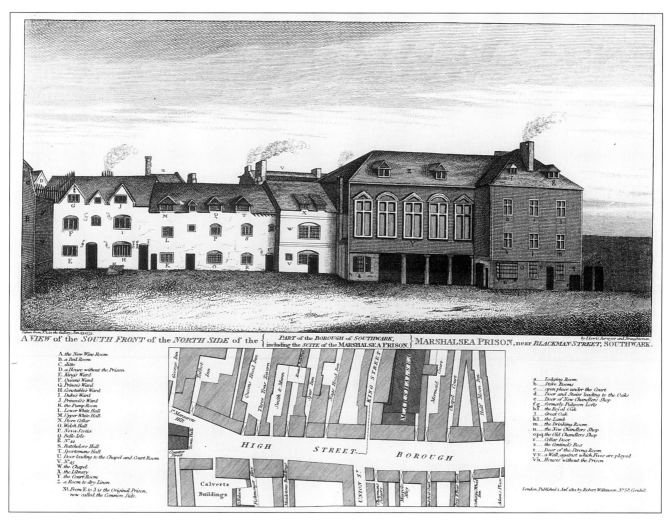

A VIEW of the SOUTH FRONT of the NORTH SIDE of the { PART of the BOROUGH of SOUTHWARK, including the SCITE of the MARSHALSEA PRISON. } MARSHALSEA PRISON, near BLACKMAN STREET, SOUTHWARK.

A. the New Wine Room.
B. a Bed Room.
C. ditto.
D. a House without the Prison.
E. Kings Ward.
F. Queens Ward.
G. Princes Ward.
H. Constables Ward.
I. Dukes Ward.
J. Princess Ward.
K. the Pump Room.
L. Lower White Hall.
M. Upper White Hall.
N. Store Cellar.
O. Welsh Hall.
P. Nova Scotia.
Q. Belle Isle.
R. No 44.
S. Batchelors Hall.
T. Sportsmans Hall.
U. Door leading to the Chapel and Court Room.
V. No 45.
W. the Chapel.
X. the Library.
Y. the Court Room.
z. a Room to dry Linen.

NB. From F. to J is the Original Prison, now called the Common Side.

a. Lodging Room.
b. Store Rooms.
c. open place under the Court.
d. Door and Stairs leading to the Oaks.
e. Door of New Chandlers Shop.
f.g. formerly Pidgeon Lofts.
h.i. the Royal Oak.
j. Great Oak.
k.l. the Lamb.
m. the Drinking Room.
n. the New Chandlers Shop.
o.p.q. the Old Chandlers Shop.
r. Cellar Door.
s. the Contracts Box.
t. Door of the Strong Room.
v.v. a Wall, against which Fives are played.
v.u. Houses without the Prison.

London, Published 1 Jul. 1812 by Robert Wilkinson, No 58, Cornhill.

his trial by the Bishop of Winchester. When Elizabeth came to the throne, Bonner, the Catholic Bishop of London, was brought here and died a prisoner in 1569. In later years, most inmates at the Marshalsea were debtors but other offenders were also incarcerated here. In the late 18th century, about 300 prisoners were held in very poor conditions and the prison was badly in need of repair. The prison was therefore moved to a site north of St George's Church. In 1811, the government purchased the White Lyon, the old county gaol of Surrey, that was on an adjacent site and a new Marshalsea was built. In 1824, Charles Dickens' father was imprisoned for debt for three months in the Marshalsea. It was closed in 1842, then used as a factory. This engraving, by Robert Wilkinson, was published in 1812, to show the new Marshalsea. The different rooms or areas of the prison are listed, including the wards, chapel, library, lodging rooms, chandler's shop and drinking rooms.

203   *(left)*
The courtyard of the Marshalsea Prison in the 18th century

204
The Borough Compter
This prison was also known as the Southwark Compter. A compter was built in the 16th century within the former parish church of St Margaret's (which also housed an assize court and an admiralty court). The Compter was used principally to hold debtors or petty offenders for the five parishes of Southwark. It was destroyed by fire in 1676 and a new

prison was built in 1717 on Mill Lane (running north from Tooley Street) in Bermondsey. This Compter was destroyed in the Gordon Riots but an enlarged prison was built on the site and is featured in this watercolour of about 1826, by G. Yates. It was converted to a female prison in 1848, closed in 1852 and demolished in 1855.

205
The Bridewell at Deptford
The regime at Bridewell (see illustrations 189-90) was copied in new gaols across the country and these also became known as 'Bridewells'. Deptford, in Kent (now in the London Borough of Lewisham) was the location of the Tudors' great naval dockyard. This view of the Bridewell dates from about 1798.

206

Horsemonger Lane Gaol, Southwark
Horsemonger Lane Gaol was built (1791-98) as the Surrey County Gaol for 400 prisoners. It was a three-storey quadrangle. Three sides were for criminals and one side for debtors. An adjacent building was a Sessions House for Surrey (later rebuilt as the large Sessions House on Newington Causeway). Executions took place outside the gaol, or on the roof. In November 1849, Charles Dickens attended the execution of Mr. and Mrs Manning, who had murdered their lodger. Horsemonger Lane Gaol was closed in 1878 and demolished in 1880. Horsemonger Lane is now named Harper Road.

207

Interior of the Chapel at Horsemonger Lane Gaol
This watercolour of the chapel, by G. Yates, dates from about 1826.

**The courtyard and Governor's
House at Tothill Fields Prison**
Westminster Bridewell was built in
1618, at the north end of present-
day Rochester Row, to hold petty
offenders and vagrants. This
Bridewell was the setting for
Hogarth's engraving of the Harlot
beating hemp (illustration 221). It
was closed in 1834 and a new Tothill
Fields Prison was erected on the
north side of Francis Street. This was
a large prison, with 549 cells, to hold
up to 900 prisoners. In 1845, it was
decided that Coldbath Fields in
Clerkenwell should hold adult male
convicts and that Tothill Fields
Prison should hold only women and
males under the age of 17. This
illustration dates from about 1850.
Tothill Fields was closed and
demolished in 1884. Westminster
Cathedral now stands on part of the
site.

209 *(above)*
Millbank Penitentiary, Westminster
Millbank Penitentiary opened in
1816. It was built, in the shape of a
six-pointed star, on marshy ground
on the north bank of the Thames
(the Tate Gallery now stands on the
site). The entrance, on Millbank,
faced the river. Its corridors were
three miles long and it had 1,000
cells. At the time, it was probably the
largest prison in England. It was
originally intended for convicts.
They were held in separate cells and
forbidden to talk to each other for
the first half of their sentence.
Pentonville Prison was opened, to
hold convicts, in 1842 and so
Millbank became an ordinary prison
and increased its capacity to about
1,500 prisoners (by the sharing of
cells). Inmates were only held for a
few months before their transfer to
other prisons, and so about 4,000 to
5,000 passed through Millbank's
gates each year. It became a military
prison in 1870, was closed in 1890
and demolished in 1903. This
engraving of 1829, based on a
drawing by Thomas Shepherd, shows
the front entrance. There was a moat
between the roadside fence and the
prison wall.

**The central tower of one of the
pentagons at Millbank Penitentiary**
This photograph shows the block for
female inmates and one of the
central towers, that gave a good view
of the yards and cell blocks. The
woman in the courtyard on the left
may be a prison nurse or perhaps a
visitor related to the photographer.

211 (right)
**Clerkenwell, from John Rocque's
map of the cities of London and
Westminster, 1746**
Clerkenwell originated as a hamlet,
to the north of the City of London,
in the 12th century near to monastic
foundations such as the Priory of St
John of Jerusalem. After the
dissolution of the monasteries, many
fine houses were built here and
population also increased as an
overspill from the crowded City
streets. In the 16th century, sessions
of the Justices of the Peace were
held in taverns but, in 1612, a
Sessions House (Hicks Hall) was

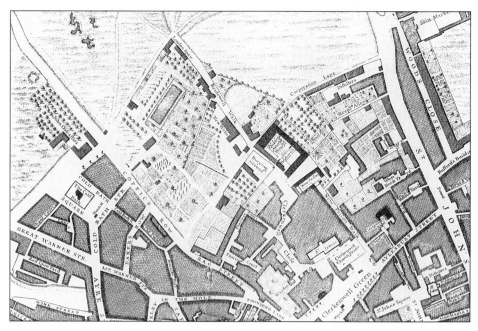

built on St John Street. In 1615, a
Bridewell was built at Clerkenwell,
for the 'punishment and
employment of the rogues and
vagabonds of Middlesex'. The
Bridewell is marked on Rocque's
map, next to the burial ground and
the Quaker workhouse. A few years
later, another prison, the 'New
Prison', was built just to the south of
the Bridewell. It was burned down by

prisoners in 1679, but repaired. It
was enlarged in 1774, to relieve
pressure on Newgate Gaol, which
was overcrowded. The Bridewell was
demolished in 1804 and, in 1818,
the New Prison was rebuilt and
enlarged (see illustration 212), to
utilise the site of the Bridewell. It
could now hold about 240 prisoners.
In 1845/6, the New Prison was again
rebuilt and renamed as the
Clerkenwell House of Detention
(illustrations 213-15), holding
prisoners on remand. It had 216
cells designed for single occupation,
but two or three prisoners might be
kept in the same cell. From 1846 to
1878, Clerkenwell House of
Detention was the busiest prison in
London, because prisoners were
held only for a short period,
awaiting trial. In 1859 alone, 5,422

men and 2,292 women passed
through the gates. It was closed in
1877 and much of it was demolished
in 1890. The remaining parts, almost
entirely underground, have been
restored and opened to the public.

212 (above)
**Interior of the New Prison,
Clerkenwell in about 1840**
This watercolour of the New Prison,
by Thomas H. Shepherd, dates from
about 1850. Conditions at the
Bridewell and the New Prison were
poor. Prisoners were crowded into
cells. The keeper of the gaol and the
gaolers extracted fees, or their last
few possessions, from the inmates
(for better cells, food, or the
opportunity for sex with other
inmates).

213   (left)
Bird's-eye view of the House of Detention, Clerkenwell, in about 1860
This is the Clerkenwell House of Detention, as rebuilt in 1845/6. The two wings in the foreground were for women. The two wings behind were for men.

214   (below right)
The gate of the House of Detention, Clerkenwell

215   (below left)
The House of Detention, Clerkenwell, after the explosion of 1867
Two leading members of the nationalist Irish Republican Brotherhood, or Fenians, were held on remand at the House of Detention in 1867. Some other Fenians attempted to free them, by blowing a hole in the prison wall. The explosion occurred on 13 December 1867. It blew a 60-ft wide hole in the wall. Nearby houses were demolished and nine people died. The Fenians did not escape and the bombers were captured. One of them, Michael Barrett, was the last man to be hanged in public outside Newgate Gaol. This illustration is from the *Illustrated London News*, showing the damage to the prison walls from inside the prison yard.

216-217   (facing page)
Two views of the House of Correction at Coldbath Fields, Clerkenwell
In 1794, a House of Correction was built in Clerkenwell, just to the north of the Bridewell and New Prison, on Coldbath Fields, to house convicted criminals. Mount Pleasant Post Office now stands on this site. Illustration 216 is an engraving, from a drawing by Thomas Shepherd, showing the gate of the House of Correction. Illustration 217 is a view of the prison, published in 1798, from the north (St Paul's Cathedral can be seen in the background). Coldbath Fields was notorious for its severity. The prisoners were not allowed to talk to each other and punishments included jobs that had no purpose (carrying cannonballs, sessions on

one of the six treadmills, or picking oakum – picking apart old ship ropes so that the fibre could be used again). A prisoner might have to work on the treadmill for three or four hours a day. Over 340 prisoners could work on the treadmills at a time. The House of Correction was known as the 'Steel', after the Bastille in Paris. In 1799, Coleridge and Southey wrote in *The Devil's Thoughts*:

As he went through Cold-Bath Fields he
    saw a solitary cell,
And the devil was pleased, for it gave him
    a hint,
For improving his prisons in Hell.

By the 1850s, about 1,450 prisoners were held at any one time at Coldbath Fields, increasing to about 1,700 in the 1870s. In 1850, female prisoners were transferred to Tothill Fields Prison and Coldbath Fields was closed in 1885.

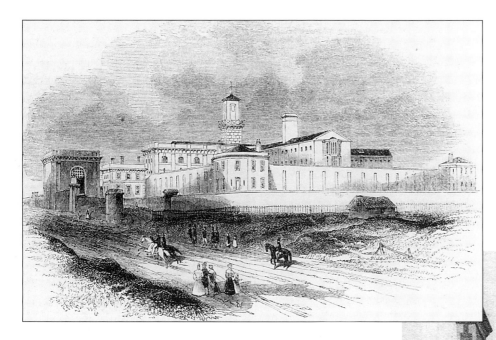

218   *(above)*

Pentonville Prison

Pentonville Prison, on Caledonian Road, Islington, opened in 1842. It was called a 'Model Prison' and built on the 'separate and silent' system. It originally held convicts prior to their transportation. It was subsequently used to hold those convicts sentenced to hard labour. A 'crank' was installed that did nothing but exhaust the inmates who had to turn it by hand. The convicts were said to 'grind the wind'. On 3 August 1916, Sir Roger Casement was hanged in Pentonville for treason. The prison presently holds about 800 prisoners. This view is from the *Illustrated London News* of 13 August 1842, at the time that it opened for business.

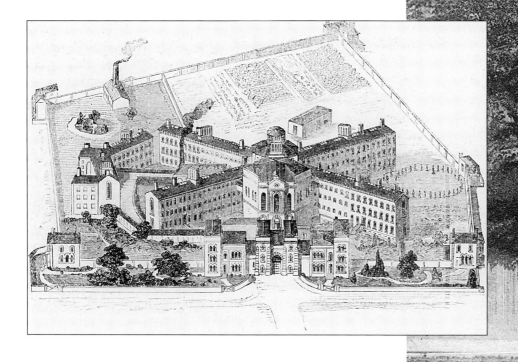

219 *(below left)*

The Surrey House of Correction, Wandsworth

Wandsworth Prison was originally a Surrey House of Correction, built in 1851 to accommodate 1,000 prisoners. The male section consisted of five wings radiating from a central building. The female part was similar but with three wings. Cranks were installed for those prisoners sentenced to hard labour. On the closure of Horsemonger Lane Gaol in 1878, Wandsworth began carrying out executions for South London crimes. William Joyce ('Lord Haw-Haw') was also executed here in January 1946. Oscar Wilde was held here for the first six months of his sentence in 1895.

220 *(below)*

Holloway Prison, *c.*1906

Holloway Prison was built for the Corporation of the City of London as a House of Correction (to replace Giltspur Street Compter and relieve pressure on Newgate). It opened in 1852 and accommodated 350 prisoners. The tower (copied from Warwick Castle) and battlements caused it to be known as 'Holloway Castle', as on this postcard. Oscar Wilde was held here in 1895, awaiting his trial. From 1903, only female prisoners were held in Holloway and it was extended to hold 975 inmates. Mrs Pankhurst and some other suffragettes were imprisoned here from 1906. The 'castle' was demolished in 1979 and a more modern prison built in its place.

XIII PUNISHMENTS IN PRISON

As if conditions in prison were not bad enough, there were punishments that could make a prisoner's sentence that little more severe. Some of these (the treadmill, the crank and picking oakum) have already been noted. There were many others – humans are very creative on this subject, and it should be remembered that torture (a subject outside the scope of this book) was an everyday occurrence in many prisons until at least the 18th century.

221 *(above)*
Hogarth's engraving of the harlot beating hemp in Westminster Bridewell
One of the inmates has had her hands placed in the stocks to the right (presumably for failing to work hard enough). The stocks bear the declaration, '*Better to Work than Stand thus*'.

222 *(top right)*
The *Justitia* hulk with convicts at work on the bank of the Thames near Woolwich
When transportation ceased, obsolete warships were used as floating prisons. The first 'hulk', the *Justitia*, was anchored in the Thames

in 1776 at Woolwich. This engraving is from the *Malefactor's Register* of that year. By 1841, there were nine hulks (holding 3,500 convicts) moored in the Thames or at Plymouth, Portsmouth, Sheerness, Chatham, Bermuda and Gibraltar. Conditions on the hulks were dreadful; death or illness from scurvy, typhus or dysentery being commonplace. The convicts on hulks also suffered badly during outbreaks of cholera. Within the first few months of use of the *Justitia*, 176 of the 632 convicts had died. Convicts might be taken ashore to work – breaking stones, carrying coal or cleaning sewers. Many convicts worked on the construction of new docks for London.

223 *(right)*
The treadmill at Brixton Prison
Brixton Prison was erected in 1820 as a House of Correction for Surrey. It was built for 175 prisoners but often held about 400 and so became one of the unhealthiest London prisons. In 1824, it was furnished with the first of the treadmills, as shown in this undated print. A treadmill was a large cylinder with steps on the outside. As prisoners stepped onto it, the treadmill began to turn and the men would have to climb onto the next step, then continue climbing, in order to remain upright. Treadmills sometimes had a useful function – perhaps grinding corn (as at Brixton) or bringing water up from a

well, but sometimes they had no function at all, except to punish the prisoners. Surrey established a new House of Correction at Wandsworth in 1851 and Brixton Prison was purchased by the Government in 1853 to hold female convicts. It was expanded so as to hold 700 prisoners and then served as a military prison from 1882 to 1898. In 1902, it became the trial and remand prison for London and the Home Counties (holding over 1,000 prisoners in 1991). It was the scene of a mass escape, by 20 prisoners, in 1973.

224 *(far right)*
The 'Boys' Pony' at the House of Correction, Coldbath Fields, Clerkenwell
This illustration is from a supplement to the *Illustrated London News* of 27 June 1874. The pony was shaped so as to make a thrashing more effective and easy to administer.

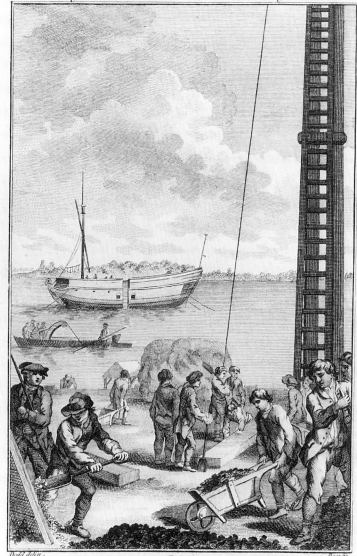

View of the **JUSTITIA HULK**, with the Convicts at Work, near Woolwich.

XIV   LAW REPORTS AND LEGAL EPHEMERA

I have included a few examples of law reports and other legal documents or ephemera in this section. Law reports are official or unofficial summaries of the result of a case and the legal principles that were applied to the facts. The Common Law has grown and developed by the combination of law reporting and a fixed hierarchy of courts, in which higher court decisions are precedents that bind lower courts for the future (unless a later case can be differentiated). New legislation results in a new body of case law, in which every sentence (indeed every word) in a statute or regulation may be analysed or argued over in the courts. The study of previous cases, and the precedents they established, therefore remains an essential part of a lawyer's work. The number of published reports increased gradually at first, but has escalated rapidly in the last two decades. Legal practitioners are now almost overwhelmed by the amount of material already available and the large number of published reports, journals, digests, textbooks, supplements and the like that flood into libraries, offices and chambers. Case reports and commentaries are also distributed on CD-ROM or by e-mail, or available 'on-line' through computers. There are some doubts as to whether this vast (perhaps excessive) flow of information is truly improving the performance of lawyers or the service received by clients.

Lawyers have always been substantial users of paper. Information is one of the keys to success in the law and paper has always been the best way to convey information. The arrival of systems for the so-called 'paperless office' does not appear to have reduced the amount of paper circulating within, or between, the courts, lawyers' offices and clients. In any event, e-mail messages and printouts of case reports from a computer do not make attractive illustrations so I can happily restrict this section to earlier times.

225
Broadsheet reporting the execution of Thomas Maynard and three others at Newgate, 1829
Broadsheets such as this were commonly produced for public hangings. They reported the offence and trial but might also include the purported last moments of the condemned – perhaps their dying speeches or, as here, a letter allegedly written by one man the night before his execution. At this time, almost 200 offences carried the death penalty. These four men had been convicted of forgery, burglary and stealing (30 sheep). They were hung on 31 December 1829, so at least the crowd had an 'entertaining' New Years Eve. The chaplain of Newgate, known as the 'Ordinary', prepared notes on the life of many of those who were to be executed. These would be sold on the day of execution and a collection of them subsequently became 'The Newgate Calendar'.

Execution,

At the ... Old Bailey,

THIS MORNING,
31 Oct. 1829

Of the 4 Unhappy Men.

THOMAS THOMAS MAYNARD was tried with *Richard Hubard Jones* and *Joseph William West*, for forging and uttering an order on the Receiving-General of the Customs for the sum of £1,973 The facts of the case were these :—On the 18th of April last, the order in question was presented for payment, & as the signatures of the three Commissioners whose names were subscribed were well imitated no suspicion was excited, and it was readily paid. The forgery, however, was very soon discovered, but although great exertoins were made, no clue could be obtained to discover the offenders, until the month of August following, when James, who was a Clerk in an office at the Custom house through which the genuine orders past, in a course for payment, was apprehended, in consequence of his having passed one of the Bank-note for £100 which had been given in payment for the forged order, & in the course of the same month, *Maynard* and *West* were apprehended at Taunton, in Somersetshire, to which place they had recently fled from London. They were proved to have been in company with *Jones* about the time when the forgery was committed, previous to which they were in great poverty, and directly after seen with large sums in their possession ; the name of THOMAS MAYNARD, which had been written by the person presenting forged order, was proved to be MAYNARD's hand-writing, and his person corresponded so exactly with that of the individual who uttered the forgery that the witness swore they believed him to be the utterer. *Jones* was found Guilty as an accessary befor the fact, and transported for sevan years. MAYNARD was capitally convicted and *West* was acquitted.

THOMAS NEWITT was tried with *Robert Dennington* and *Wm. Williams* for stealing thirty sheep. On the trial it appeared that on the night of the 2d of August, the sheep in question were placed in one of the pens in a field belonging to a Mr. Thompson, in Liverpool-road, Islington, from which place they were to be conveyed to Smithfield Market on the following morning. They were safe at twelve o'Clock that night. but at the usual hour of removing cattle to the Market they were missing—the next day they were traced to the possession of the prisoners- and it was proved that they were slaughtered by *Dennington and Williams*, by the direction of *Newitt*, Many facts of a circumstantial nature were also given in evidence, that fully established the guilt of the prisoners, all of whom were convicted. *Newitt* was *formerly a Butcher* & resided in Church-lane, in the Strand. where he amassed a little property, but a course of dissipation and drunkness quickly reduced him to a case of beggary. He was frequently brought up to Bow-street, charg'd with assaulting his wife. and was in the habit of treating t r with

great cruelty at the time of his Trialhe was in a very bad state of Health, but he has since perfectly recovered.

STEPHEN SANDFORD & Wm. LISLIE was convicted for a Burglary in the Dwelling House of MR. STULTZ a Tailor in Bond-street The Prosecutor's House was broke open about 2 o'Clock in the morning, of the day stated in the indictment, and an alarm being given, the Prisoners were seen running away by Bannester, a Watchman, who called to them to stop SANDFORD, presented a Pistol at him, which missed fire,—They were both apprehended at a short distance from the Prosecutor's House, SANDFORD was also tried and convicted of attempting tot Murder the Watchman.

The following Letter written by One the unhappy Sufferers the Night before his execution

"My dear Friend.   Newgate. Dec. 30, 1829,

'Did you but know the feelings I possess at this moment you would shed the tender tear of pity for me. When I reflect on the respectability of my friends and the situation they obtained for me, my heart is ready to burst with ingratitude but to support idleness and extravagance, I did that act, for which my life is become forfeited. Let the last prayers of a deluded man be offered for your prosperity avoid the paths of sin and particularly be aware of the many t mptations held out by those which has effected my ruin. Offer the sprit of consolation to my afflicted parents and relatives ; may they soon forget the ignominy I have cast up on the family by my shameful death, and I hope the finger of scorn may never be pointed to them in dirision of my wretched fate. Farewell my beloved friend may the poor advice I have offered. be accepted, and that you may be a useful member of that society, of which I have disgraced.

'Is the last wish of your wretched friend.

This morning at the usual hour these unhappy men were conducted to the fatal spot and in a short time launched into eternity

COPY OF VERSES.

Good people all were are you be
   Draw near awhile and list to me
While unto you *I* will relate
These four unhappy peoples fate,

This morn upon the gallows high
Four fine young men alas did die
Oh! think how dreadful is their doom
Cut off in prime of manhoods bloom

To see them in their dreary cells
No pen can write no tongue can tell
The agonies th er did endure
Will cause your hearts to ache I'm sure

They wrung their hand while in despair
Ere' on the drop they did appear
We are doom'd to die yet ue're the las
We own the awful doom is just

So now good people one and all
A warning take by our downfall
Think on our sad unhappy fate
And mend your Lives e're it is too late.

Thomas Newitt with three young men
Their Lives did on the gallows end
Aloud for mercy they did call
May GOD above receive them all,

Printed by CARPUE & SON, Rose Lane Spitalfields.   (Hawkers Supplied)

Extracts from the *Law List* of 1856
This is the title page from the 1856 *Law List*, with the first pages of the lists of Judges and Attorneys. The *Law List* naturally included barristers but also, at this time, listed the Advocates and Proctors of the ecclesiastical and Admiralty courts.

CORRECTED TO JAN. 1ST, 1856.

THE LAW LIST;

BEING A LIST OF THE

JUDGES AND OFFICERS

OF THE DIFFERENT

Courts of Justice:

COUNSEL,

WITH THE DATES OF THEIR CALL AND INNS OF COURT:

SPECIAL PLEADERS, CONVEYANCERS;

AND THE

ONLY AUTHENTIC AND COMPLETE LIST OF CERTIFICATED

ATTORNEYS, NOTARIES, &c.,

IN ENGLAND AND WALES,

WITH THE

London Agents to the Country Attorneys,

As printed by Permission of the Commissioners of Inland Revenue.

TO WHICH ARE ADDED,

THE CIRCUITS, JUDGES, CLERKS, AND HIGH BAILIFFS

OF THE

COUNTY COURTS.

LAW AND PUBLIC OFFICERS, CIRCUITS OF THE JUDGES, TABLE OF SHERIFFS AND AGENTS,	LONDON COMMISSIONERS FOR TAKING OATHS IN CHANCERY, QUARTER SESSIONS, &c., &c.

AND A VARIETY OF OTHER USEFUL MATTERS.

BY WILLIAM POWELL,

OF THE INLAND REVENUE OFFICE, SOMERSET-HOUSE,

REGISTRAR OF CERTIFICATES.

LONDON:

V. & R. STEVENS AND G. S. NORTON,

Law Booksellers and Publishers,

(Successors to the late J. & W. T. CLARKE, of Portugal Street,)

26, BELL YARD, LINCOLN'S INN.

1856.

Notice.—*The Law List is made up and closed to the 1st of January in each year.*

Price 6s. 6d. neatly bound.

Judges.]   [xii]   [THE LAW LIST.

JUDGES.

Lord High Chancellor:
Right Hon. Robert Monsey Rolfe, Lord Cranworth, 40, upper brook-st. grosvenor-square, and Cranworth, Norfolk.

Master of the Rolls:
Right Hon. Sir John Romilly, knt. 6, hyde-park-terrace

Lords Justices:
Right Hon. Sir J. L. Knight-Bruce, knt. roehampton-priory
Right Hon. Sir George James Turner, knt. 23, park-crescent regent's-park

Vice-Chancellors:
Right Hon. Sir Richard Torin Kindersley, knt. 18, hyde-park-square.
Hon. Sir John Stuart, knt. 19, hertford-street, mayfair
Hon. Sir William Page Wood, knt. 13, great george-street, westminster

Queen's Bench:
Right Honourable John Lord Campbell, stratheden-house, knightsbridge
Sir J. T. Coleridge, knt. 26, park-crescent, regent's-park
Sir Wm. Wightman, knt. 38, eaton-place, belgrave-square
Sir William Erle, knt. 4, park-crescent, regent's-park
Sir Charles Crompton, knt. 22, hyde-park-square

Common Pleas:
Right Hon. Sir John Jervis, knt. 47, eaton-square
Sir C. Cresswell, knt. 21, prince's-gate, knightsbridge
Sir Edward Vaughan Williams, knt. 1, park-st. westminster
Sir Richard Budden Crowder, knt. 17, carlton-house-terrace
Sir James Shaw Willes, knt. 16, eaton-square

Exchequer:
Right Honourable Sir F. J. Pollock, knt. queen-square-house, guilford-st.
Sir Ed. Hall Alderson, knt. 9, park-crescent, portland-place
Sir Thomas Joshua Platt, knt. 59, portland-place
Sir Samuel Martin, knt. 79, eaton-place, belgrave-square
Sir George William Bramwell, knt. 3 old palace-yard, westmr.

Court of Appeals in Bankruptcy:
Right Hon. Sir J. L. Knight-Bruce, knt. roehampton-priory
Right Hon. Sir George James Turner, knt. 23, park-crescent regent's-park

---

THE PROCEEDINGS

AT THE

SESSIONS of PEACE, Oyer and Terminer,

FOR THE

CITY of LONDON,

AND

County of MIDDLESEX,

ON

WEDNESDAY the 6th, THURSDAY the 7th, FRIDAY the 8th, SATURDAY the 9th, and MONDAY the 11th of *September*;

In the 12th Year of His MAJESTY's Reign,

BEING THE

Seventh SESSIONS in the MAYORALTY

OF THE

Right Honourable Sir *John Barnard*, Knight,

LORD-MAYOR of the CITY of *LONDON*.

For the YEAR 1738.

NUMBER VII.

LONDON:

Printed for J. ROBERTS, at the *Oxford-Arms* in *Warwick-Lane*.

M.DCC.XXXVIII.   (Price Three-Pence.)

N. B. *The Public may be assured, that (during the Mayoralty of the Right Honourable Sir JOHN BARNARD, Lord-Mayor of this City) the Sessions-Book will be constantly sold for Three-Pence, and no more; and shall contain the usual Quantity sold for Six-Pence for many Years past: And also that the whole Account of every Sessions shall be carefully compriz'd in One such Three-penny Book, without any farther Burthen to the Purchasers.*

THE PROCEEDINGS

AT THE

Sessions of the Peace, and Oyer and Terminer,

For the CITY of *LONDON*, &c.

BEFORE the Right Honourable Sir JOHN BARNARD, Knt. Lord-Mayor of the City of *London*; the Worshipful Mr. Justice PAGE; SIMON URLIN, Esq; Deputy-Recorder of the City of *London*, and Others his Majesty's Justices of Oyer and Terminer for the City of *London*, and Justices of Goal-Delivery of *Newgate*, holden for the said City and County of *Middlesex*.

London Jury:	Middlesex Jury:
James Crawforth,	* Thomas Nichols,
William Williams,	Ralph Mayo,
John Mason,	Daniel Weedon,
Robert Lane,	Edmund Franklin,
Robert Johnson,	Thomas Bromely,
Richard Pepys,	† Thomas Franklin,
John Barlow,	John Mayo,
Richard Peddy,	Henry Brisbow,
John Forward,	Jonathan Pateman,
Benjamin Haslop,	Charles Thompson,
Samuel Sacheverel,	John Whitehead,
John Moore.	Thomas Finch.

1. Charlotte Markson, was indicted (with Levi Abram, not taken) for stealing three Mens Hats, value 36 s. the Goods of *John Browning*, in the Parish of St. *Bennet Fink*, *July* 6. Guilty 4 s. 10 d.

2. Mary Spalding, of St. *Butolph Bishopsgate*, was indicted for stealing 21 *Legborn* Hats, value 3 s. and 4 Straw Hats, value 12 d. the Goods of *John Clark*, *June* 13. Guilty.

3. John Miles, was indicted for stealing a cloth Coat and Waistcoat, val. 16 s. a Man's Hat, val. 4 s. a light natural Wig, val. 4 s. and a Silver Watch, val. 50 s. the Goods of *Richard Bootes*, in the dwelling House of *Thomas Bowen*, in the Parish of St. *Stephen Coleman-Street*, *July* 5. Guilty 39 s.

4. John Collins, of St. *Dunstan in the East*, was indicted for stealing a Frail of Raisins, value 5 s. the Goods of *Thomas Chitty*, *July* 19. Guilty.

5. Joseph Upton, of St. *Butolph Bishopsgate*, was indicted for breaking and entering the House of *Robert Allen*, between the Hours of One and Two, in the Night, with intent to steal the Money and Goods of the said *Allen*, *July* 12.

Mr *Allen.* I was call'd up between 1 and 2 o'Clock in the Night, the 12th of *July* last, by a Neighbour's Servant, who is a *Baker*, and lives over-against my House. I look'd out of my Chamber Window, and he told me, somebody had been breaking into my Cellar. I desir'd him to watch, 'till I could come down; and when I came to examine the Cellar Door, I found one of the Bolts broke, and the Staples that belong'd to the other, were broke likewise. I had order'd my Servant to fasten them about Eight o'Clock; which he did; for after I had been out, to take a Pint of Beer, I return'd Home, and about Nine, I saw them both fast. When I found the Door broke open, I order'd my Servant to search the Cellar;

† Richard Burnet, was on Thursday sworn in the Room of Thomas Franklin.
* Thomas Nichols was ill on Saturday, and John Freeman was sworn the rest of the Time.

A NEW, COMPLETE, AND ACCURATE

LIST

OF ALL THE

CERTIFICATED ATTORNEYS

RESIDING IN

ONDON, WESTMINSTER, AND BOROUGH OF
SOUTHWARK, AND THEIR ENVIRONS;

PRINTED FROM THE STAMP-OFFICE LISTS.

CE.—Offices, Appointments, &c.—In future all Offices, Appointments
Description, which are inserted in the present year's LAW LIST as held by
orneys, will be repeated in the next year's LAW LIST, unless they are altered
e slip or ticket delivered at the Stamp Office on renewing the Certificate
he next year.

e marked thus* are Members of the Incorporated Law Society of
United Kingdom, by Charters of Wm. IV. and Victoria;——
he Metropolitan and Provincial Law Association;—— ‡ the
w Association for the Benefit of Widows and Families of
ofessional Men in the Metropolis and its Vicinity;—— ‖ the
stices' Clerks' Society.——The "London Commissioners to
minister Oaths in Chancery" are thus distinguished : " Com.
ths in Chy.," and see alphabetical list, post. *⁎*For Per-
ual Commissioners in LONDON, see post.

OT, William, and Wm. Abbot, jun. (firm Abbot & Sons),
·ctors and notaries, doctors'-commons
ott, Chas. James (firm Jenkins & Abbott), 8, new-inn
tt, Francis Geo., com. oaths in chy. (firm Abbott & Wheatly),
a, southampton-buildings, chan.-lane, and staines, middlesex
tent agents)
t, George Washington, and Joseph Seymour Salaman
m Abbott & Salaman), 13, basinghall-street, city
Francis Gibbs, att. and not., att. of insolvent debtors ct.,
in bankruptcy, and com. for affidvts. 15, addington-square,
berwell-road, and colchester, essex
t, Isaac, 6, newcastle-st. strand, and 1, christopher-street,
ton-garden
ham, George Frederick, com. oaths in chy., 6, great marlbo-
gh-street, westminster, and kentish-town
iams, Michael, 23. southampton-buildings, chancery-lane
iams, Samuel, 4, lincoln's-inn-fields, and 32, aberdeen-place,
da-hill
iams, Samuel Benjamin, 27, bloomsbury-square
i, William, 46, upper bedford-place, russell-square
G

REPORTS

OF

CASES

DECIDED IN THE

HIGH COURT OF CHANCERY,

BY

THE RIGHT HON. SIR ANTHONY HART,

AND

THE RIGHT HON. SIR LAUNCELOT SHADWELL,

VICE-CHANCELLORS OF ENGLAND.

BY NICHOLAS SIMONS,

Of Lincoln's Inn, Esq. Barrister at Law.

VOL. II.

1827, 1828 & 1829.

LONDON:
J. & W. T. CLARKE,
LAW BOOKSELLERS AND PUBLISHERS,
PORTUGAL-STREET, LINCOLN'S-INN.

1831.

---

24 CASES IN CHANCERY.

BURTON v. HODSOLL.

1827:
24th July and
29th October.

Will.
Construction.
Conversion.
Escheat.

Testator gave
a Copyhold Es-
tate to Trustees
for his Wife,
until the Leases
to which it was
subject expired,
and directed that
then it should
be sold, and the
Proceeds be in-
vested for the
benefit of his
Children ; but,
if his Wife
should die be-
fore the Leases
expired, that it
should be imme-
diately sold, and
the Proceeds
disposed of as
before. The
Wife survived
the Children,
but died before
the Leases ex-
pired. The sur-
viving Trustee,
who claimed the
Estate for his

THOMAS LAMBE made his Will, dated the 21st
of June 1804, and which was, in part, as follows :
" I give and devise unto *John Hodsoll,* of *Carey-street,*
Stone Mason, and the Survivor of them, or
the Executors or Administrators of such Survivor, all
those my three Freehold Messuages in *Furnival's-Inn-
Court, Holborn,* and also all my Stock or Shares in
any of the Public Funds, and all Money in hand, or
Debts due to me, to be placed in the Three per Cent
Consolidated Bank of *England,* whereof I may be pos-
sessed of or entitled to, upon this special Trust and
Confidence, that they my said Trustees shall and do
permit and suffer my Wife, *Maria Dove Lambe,* to
receive and take, for and during the term of her natural
life, all Rents and Profits of my said Messuages, and
all other Freeholds or Leaseholds that I may be pos-
sessed of, and the Interest, Dividends and Proceeds of
the said Stock or Shares in the Bank of *England,* except the Presents hereinafter mentioned, for the support
and maintenance of Herself and all my legitimate Issue
which I now have or may hereafter have by her, except
as follows ; that is to say, that in case my reputed Son,
known by the name of *Thomas Lambe,* shall live to
attain the age of Twenty-one years, I will and direct that
they my said Trustees shall and do, with all convenient

own benefit, was decreed to surrender it to the Administrator of the
Children, but without prejudice to the Rights of the customary Heirs of
either the Testator or the Children, if any such Heirs were in existence.

---

227 *(left)*

Two pages from 'The Proceedings at the Sessions of Peace, Oyer and Terminer for the City of London and Middlesex' in September 1738

This series of reports, by journalists and lawyers, of the proceedings at the Sessions House at Old Bailey, and later at the Central Criminal Court, was very popular. The reports were produced as pamphlets from the late 17th century. The reports listed the defendants brought before the court, their crimes, the jurors, the verdict and any sentence. They also recounted some of the evidence, sometimes setting almost verbatim the statements made by important witnesses or the defendants themselves. This extract, from an issue covering the proceedings of 6-11 September 1738, includes a note of the case of John Miles, found guilty of stealing a coat, wig and silver watch. It also reports that Joseph Upton was indicted for breaking into the house of Robert Allen. The evidence given by Allen is then set out.

228

Law Reports: a case in the Court of Chancery in 1827

One great advantage of English Common Law over many other systems is that the law can adapt to the times. Judges are entitled to apply the wording of old statutes and old reported cases in such a way as to take account of changing fashions, morality and new developments in technology. The basis for such a system is the accurate reporting of decided cases. The development of accurate law reporting has therefore been a vital factor in the development of the law over the

centuries. Most lawyers regularly use the modern law reports, now published weekly or monthly in a bewildering number of series or editions. However, many are less familiar with the older reports, stretching back to medieval times. Readers who are not lawyers may not have seen a law report before. I have therefore chosen a published report of 1827 for this illustration. It is the legal principle rather than the facts that matter to lawyers, but this case concerned the terms of the will of 21 June 1804 of Thomas Lambe and the leasehold properties that he had held in Furnival's Inn Court.

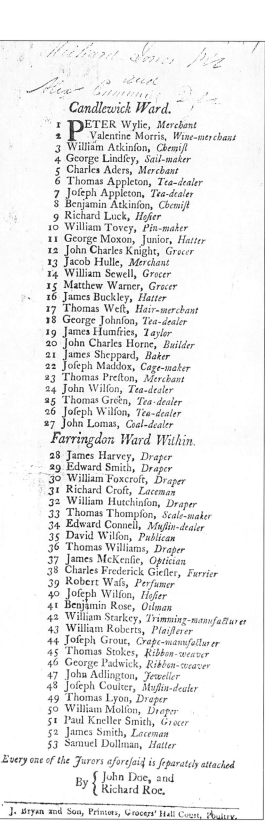

OH! DID HE!

Candlewick Ward.

1 PETER Wylie, *Merchant*
2 Valentine Morris, *Wine-merchant*
3 William Atkinson, *Chemist*
4 George Lindsey, *Sail-maker*
5 Charles Aders, *Merchant*
6 Thomas Appleton, *Tea-dealer*
7 Joseph Appleton, *Tea-dealer*
8 Benjamin Atkinson, *Chemist*
9 Richard Luck, *Hosier*
10 William Tovey, *Pin-maker*
11 George Moxon, Junior, *Hatter*
12 John Charles Knight, *Grocer*
13 Jacob Hulle, *Merchant*
14 William Sewell, *Grocer*
15 Matthew Warner, *Grocer*
16 James Buckley, *Hatter*
17 Thomas West, *Hair-merchant*
18 George Johnson, *Tea-dealer*
19 James Humfries, *Taylor*
20 John Charles Horne, *Builder*
21 James Sheppard, *Baker*
22 Joseph Maddox, *Cage-maker*
23 Thomas Preston, *Merchant*
24 John Wilson, *Tea-dealer*
25 Thomas Green, *Tea-dealer*
26 Joseph Wilson, *Tea-dealer*
27 John Lomas, *Coal-dealer*

Farringdon Ward Within.

28 James Harvey, *Draper*
29 Edward Smith, *Draper*
30 William Foxcroft, *Draper*
31 Richard Croft, *Laceman*
32 William Hutchinson, *Draper*
33 Thomas Thompson, *Scale-maker*
34 Edward Connell, *Muslin-dealer*
35 David Wilson, *Publican*
36 Thomas Williams, *Draper*
37 James McKensie, *Optician*
38 Charles Frederick Giesler, *Furrier*
39 Robert Wass, *Perfumer*
40 Joseph Wilson, *Hosier*
41 Benjamin Rose, *Oilman*
42 William Starkey, *Trimming-manufacturer*
43 William Roberts, *Plaisterer*
44 Joseph Grout, *Crape-manufacturer*
45 Thomas Stokes, *Ribbon-weaver*
46 George Padwick, *Ribbon-weaver*
47 John Adlington, *Jeweller*
48 Joseph Coulter, *Muslin-dealer*
49 Thomas Lyon, *Draper*
50 William Molson, *Draper*
51 Paul Kneller Smith, *Grocer*
52 James Smith, *Laceman*
53 Samuel Dollman, *Hatter*

Every one of the Jurors aforesaid is separately attached

By { John Doe, and
     { Richard Roe.

J. Bryan and Son, Printers, Grocers' Hall Court, Poultry.

229
A list of jurors from two wards of the City of London for a case in the Court of King's Bench in 1816

This document lists 53 of the men who were empanelled as jurors for the Court of King's Bench in 1816 (women were ineligible for jury service at that time). A jury would be chosen from this list for each case. In 1816, many more civil cases were heard by a jury. Today, most civil cases are heard by a Judge alone; one well-known exception being cases of libel or slander.

230
'Oh! Did he!'

An Edwardian postcard – note the barrister's pupil or clerk lurking at the doorway, listening to the saucy details of the case.

231
The advertisement for the Carbolic Smoke Ball

This is the advertisement that resulted in the famous case of 'Carlill v. The Carbolic Smoke Ball Company' in 1893. The sum of £100 was offered to anyone who contracted influenza after using the Carbolic Smoke Ball. Carlill did so. The court had to consider whether the advertisement was a binding offer to anyone who read it, so that the offer could then be accepted by anyone who purchased and used the smoke ball. Alternatively, was the offer to pay £100 a mere puff – that is, an advertiser's non-contractual claims about the product upon which no-one could rely if the goods did not perform as promised? The court found in favour of Carlill. This result can be seen as an early acceptance by the courts that the consumer deserved protection from the world of commerce.

CARBOLIC SMOKE BALL

WILL POSITIVELY CURE

COUGHS Cured in 1 week	**CATARRH** Cured in 1 to 3 months.	**HOARSENESS** Cured in 12 hours.	**THROAT DEAFNESS** Cured in 1 to 3 months.	**INFLUENZA** Cured in 24 hours.	**CROUP** Relieved in 5 minutes.
COLD IN THE HEAD Cured in 12 hours.	**ASTHMA** Relieved in 10 minutes.	**LOSS OF VOICE** Fully restored.	**SNORING** Cured in 1 week.	**HAY FEVER** Cured in every case.	**WHOOPING COUGH** Relieved the first application.
COLD ON THE CHEST Cured in 12 hours.	**BRONCHITIS** Cured in every case.	**SORE THROAT** Cured in 12 hours.	**SORE EYES** Cured in 2 weeks.	**HEADACHE** Cured in 10 minutes.	**NEURALGIA** Cured in 10 minutes.

As all the Diseases mentioned above proceed from one cause, they can be Cured by this Remedy.

£100 REWARD

WILL BE PAID BY THE

CARBOLIC SMOKE BALL CO.

to any Person who contracts the Increasing Epidemic,

INFLUENZA,

Colds, or any Diseases caused by taking Cold, after having used the **CARBOLIC SMOKE BALL** according to the printed directions supplied with each Ball.

£1000 IS DEPOSITED

with the ALLIANCE BANK, Regent Street, showing our sincerity in the matter.

During the last epidemic of **INFLUENZA** many thousand **CARBOLIC SMOKE BALLS** were sold as preventives against this disease, and in no ascertained case was the disease contracted by those using the **CARBOLIC SMOKE BALL.**

Free Trials at our Consulting Rooms.

For Inhalation Only.

THE CARBOLIC SMOKE BALL,

TESTIMONIALS.

The DUKE OF PORTLAND writes : "I am much obliged for the Carbolic Smoke Ball which you have sent me, and which I find most efficacious."

SIR FREDERICK MILNER, Bart., M.P., writes from Nice. March 7, 1890 ; "Lady Milner and my children have derived much benefit from the Carbolic Smoke Ball."

Lady MOSTYN writes from Carshalton, Cary Crescent, Torquay, Jan. 10, 1890 : "Lady Mostyn believes the Carbolic Smoke Ball to be a certain check and a cure for a cold, and will have great pleasure in recommending it to her friends. Lady Mostyn hopes the Carbolic Smoke Ball will have all the success its merits deserve."

Lady ERSKINE writes from Spratton Hall, Northampton, Jan. 1, 1890 : "Lady Erskine is pleased to say that the Carbolic Smoke Ball has given every satisfaction ; she considers it a very good invention."

Mrs. GLADSTONE writes : "She finds the Carbolic Smoke Ball has done her a great deal of good."

Madame ADELINA PATTI writes : "Madame Patti has found the Carbolic Smoke Ball very beneficial, and the only thing that would enable her to rest well at night when having a severe cold."

AS PRESCRIBED BY

SIR MORELL MACKENZIE, M.D.,

HAS BEEN SUPPLIED TO

H.I.M. THE GERMAN EMPRESS.

H R H. The Duke of Edinburgh, K.G.
H R H. The Duke of Connaught, K.G.
The Duke of Fife, K T.
The Marquis of Salisbury, K.G.
The Duke of Argyll, K.T.
The Duke of Westminster, K.G.
The Duke of Richmond and Gordon, K.G.
The Duke of Manchester.
The Duke of Newcastle.
The Duke of Norfolk.
The Duke of Rutland, K.G.
The Duke of Wellington.
The Marquis of Ripon, K.G.
The Earl of Derby, K.G.
Earl Spencer, K.G.
The Lord Chancellor.
The Lord Chief Justice.
Lord Tennyson.

TESTIMONIALS.

The BISHOP OF LONDON writes : "The Carbolic Smoke Ball has benefited me greatly."

The MARCHIONESS DE SAIN writes from Padworth House, Reading, Jan. 13, 1890 : "The Marchioness de Sain has daily used the Smoke Ball since the commencement of the epidemic of Influenza, and has not taken the Influenza, although surrounded by those suffering from it."

Dr. J. RUSSELL HARRIS, M.D., writes from 6, Adam Street, Adelphi, Sept. 24, 1891 : "Many obstinate cases of post-nasal catarrh, which have resisted other treatment, have yielded to your Carbolic Smoke Ball."

A. GIBBONS, Esq., Editor of the *Lady's Pictorial*, writes from 172. Strand, W.C., Feb. 14, 1890 : "During a recent sharp attack of the prevailing epidemic I had none of the unpleasant and dangerous catarrh and bronchial symptoms. I attribute this entirely to the use of the Carbolic Smoke Ball."

The Rev. Dr. CHICHESTER A. W. READE, LL.D., D.C.L., writes from Banstead Downs, Surrey, May 1890 : "My duties in a large public institution have brought me daily, during the recent epidemic of influenza, in close contact with the disease. I have been perfectly free from any symptom by having the Smoke Ball always handy. It has also wonderfully improved my voice for speaking and singing."

The Originals of these Testimonials may be seen at our Consulting Rooms, with hundreds of others.

One **CARBOLIC SMOKE BALL** will last a family several months, making it the cheapest remedy in the world at the price—10s., post free.

The **CARBOLIC SMOKE BALL** can be refilled, when empty, at a cost of 5s., post free. Address:

CARBOLIC SMOKE BALL CO., 27, PRINCES ST., HANOVER SQ., LONDON, W.

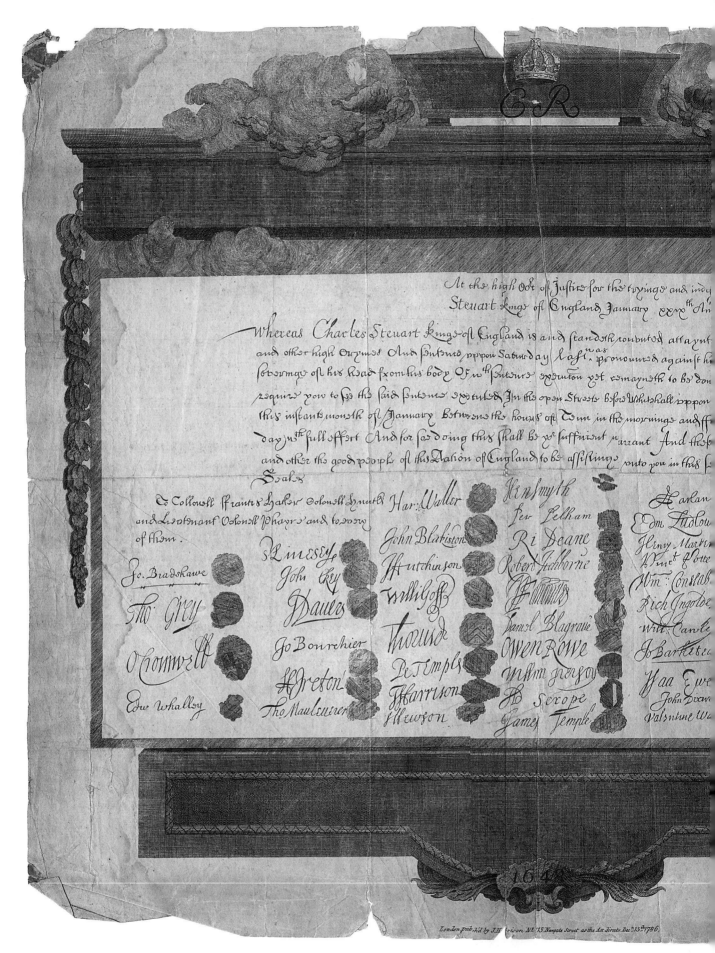

THE
INDICTMENT, ARRAIGNMENT,
TRYAL, and JUDGMENT, at large,
Of Twenty-nine
REGICIDES,
THE
Murtherers
Of His Moſt
SACRED MAJESTY
King *CHARLES* the Iſt,
Of Glorious Memory:

Begun at *Hicks's-Hall* on *Tueſday* the Ninth of *October*, 1660. and continued at the *Seſſions-Houſe* in the *Old-Baily* until *Friday* the Nineteenth of the ſame Month.

Together with a SUMMARY of the Dark and Horrid *Decrees* of thoſe *Cabbaliſts*, Preparatory to that Helliſh Fact.

Expos'd to *View* for the Reader's *Satisfaction*, and *Information* of Poſterity.

To which is added,
Their Speeches. With a Preface, giving an Account of the Riſe and Progreſs of Enthuſiaſm among us, and in other Parts of *Europe:* With the Characters, and Anſwer to the Tenets of the ſeveral Perſons Executed.

LONDON: Printed for *J. Walthoe*, *J. Knapton*, R. *Knaplock*, G. *Conyers*, *J.* and B. *Sprint*, D. *Midwinter*, B. *Lintot*, B. *Cowſe*, W. and *J. Innys*, R. *Robinſon*, T. *Wotton*, S. *Tooke*, and B. *Motte*. MDCCXXIV.

232
A death sentence on a King: January 1648/9
Charles I was tried at Westminster Hall in 1648, accused of treason for levying war against Parliament and the Kingdom of England. The trial lasted four days and 68 men served as a jury. Charles was sentenced to death and executed on 20 January 1649. The identity of the executioner is uncertain. The original warrant for Charles' death is kept in the House of Lords.

233
An account of the indictment and trial of the Regicides
This is the title page of a lengthy report, published in 1724, of the trial of the regicides at Hick's Hall (the predecessor of Clerkenwell Sessions House) in October 1660. Colonel Thomas Harrison and seven other Regicides were executed at Charing Cross.

Bibliography

— *Old Serjeants' Inn, Chancery Lane* (The Law Union and Rock Insurance Company, 1912)

— *Legal London; an exhibition in the Great Hall of the Royal Courts of Justice, London, 30 June to 30 July 1971* (1971)

— *Notable Londoners; an illustrated who's who of professional and business men* (Whitehall Publishing Co. Ltd., 1924)

— *Who Was Who*: vol.I 1897-1915, vol.II 1916-28 and vol.III 1929-40 (A & C Black)

Adcock, St John, *Wonderful London; the world's greatest city described by its best writers and pictured by its finest photographers* (*circa* 1925-29)

Baildon, W. Paley, *The Quin-Centenary of Lincoln's Inn 1422-1922* (Lincoln's Inn and Country Life, 1923)

Baker, J.H., *The Order of Serjeants at Law* (Selden Society, 1984)

Barker, F. and Jackson, P., *London, 2,000 years of a city and its people* (Cassell, 1974)

Birks, M., *Gentlemen of the Law* (Stevens & Sons, 1960)

Blackham, R.J., *London for ever, the sovereign city; its romance; its reality* (Sampson Low, Marston & Co. Ltd., n.d.)

Blackham, R.J., *Wig and gown; the story of the Temple, Gray's and Lincoln's Inn* (Sampson Low, Marston & Co. Ltd., n.d.)

Burford, E.J., *A short history of the Clink Prison* (n.d.)

Byrne, R., *Prisons and punishments of London* (Harrap, 1989)

Carr, C., *Pension Book of Clement's Inn* (Selden Society, 1960)

Chancellor, E. Beresford, *The annals of Fleet Street, its traditions and associations* (Chapman & Hall, 1912)

Daniel, T., *The Lawyers – the Inns of Court: the home of the Common Law* (Wildy & Sons, 1976)

Foss, E., *Biographia Juridica, a biographical dictionary of the Judges of England from the Conquest to the present time, 1066-1870* (John Murray, 1870)

Herber, M., *Clandestine marriages in the Chapel and Rules of the Fleet Prison 1680-1754; vols.1 and 2* (Francis Boutle Publishers, 1998-9)

Hooper, W. Eden, *The history of Newgate and the Old Bailey and a survey of the Fleet Prison and Fleet marriages, the Marshalsea and other old London Jails. With extensive remarks on crime and punishment in England from mediaeval times to the present day* (Underwood Press Ltd., 1935)

Keenlyside, H., *Allen & Overy; the firm, 1930-1998* (Allen & Overy, 1999)

Kent, William, *An Encyclopedia of London* (J.M. Dent & Sons, rev. ed. 1951)

Kirk, H., *Portrait of a profession, a history of the Solicitor's Profession, 1100 to the present day* (Oyez Publishing, 1976)

Megarry, Sir Robert, *Inns ancient and modern; a topographical and historical introduction to the Inns of Court, Inns of Chancery and Serjeants' Inn* (Selden Society, 1972)

Roxburgh, R., *The origins of Lincoln's Inn* (Cambridge University Press, 1963)

Shepherd, T.H. and Elmes, J., *London and its environs in the nineteenth century, illustrated by a series of views from original drawings by Thomas H. Shepherd with historical, topographical and critical notices* (Jones & Co., 1829)

Squibb, G.D., *Doctors' commons, a history of the College of Advocates and Doctors of Law* (Oxford University Press, 1977)

Thornbury, W. and Walford, E., *Old and New London: a narrative of its history, its people and its places* (Cassell, Petter, Calpin & Co., 1873-78)

Weinreb, B. and Hibbert, C., *The London Encyclopaedia* (Macmillan, rev. ed. 1993)

Welch, C. and Pike, W.T., *London at the opening of the Twentieth Century and Contemporary biographies* (W.T. Pike & Co., 1905)

Williams, E., *Staple Inn; customs house, wool court & Inn of Chancery; its mediaeval surroundings & associations* (Constable, 1906)

Williamson, J.B., *The history of the Temple, London from the institution of the order of the Knights of the Temple to the close of the Stuart period* (John Murray, 1924)

Whitmore, R., *Victorian and Edwardian Crime and Punishment* (Batsford, 1978)

Worsfold, T.C., *Staple Inn and its story* (Henry Bumpus, 1903)

Index